The Ancestors Within Journal

A Family Keepsake

&

Companion Guide

by the Authors of *The Ancestors Within*

First Published in the United States of America First Printing: November 2021

ISBN: 978-0-578-31847-9
Written by Amy Gillespie Dougherty
(AmyGillespie.com)

Cover Art by Celeste Walton
Cover Design by Mario Lampic

Facebook Group: "The Ancestors Within Community"

Editing and layout by Cheri Colburn
(CheriColburn@gmail.com)

This journal has been completed by

____

during the following dates

____

and with the following dedication and intention:

____

____

____

DEDICATION

To all of the fathers and all of the mothers who have brought us into this world, in whatever way and under whatever circumstances. You were the only way we got here. You are the magical link between our lives and our unique ancestry. Thank you for that one moment of creation!

Our ancestors have waited our whole lives for THIS moment!

…and our next!

PREFACE

At first, I envisioned this journal as a simple companion to the first two volumes of *The Ancestors Within*. When the authors started submitting their journal prompts, my vision for the journal changed. I started to see that it could become a family heirloom, like a treasure chest of ancestral experiences.

My interest in ancestry began when I was a child. I was adopted, and my adopted family was my only family from the time I was placed through Catholic Charities as a baby. So, for many years, my ancestors were elusive at best. My parents made sure I spent time with my grandparents, which was a blessing. I felt very connected with my grandparents and learned different things from each of them. One grandma taught me to thread a needle, while the other taught me to cane chairs. One grandpa told me stories of WWI, while the other made me sit still at the sale barn as we bought and sold sheep.

Still, I wondered at my genetics. Why did I have two different-colored eyes? Where did I get my gift for writing and music? Where did I get my love for animals and my desire to grow up to be a veterinarian? I had questions, and it wasn't until I met my birthparents and genetic family and ancestors, that I came to the realization that I had spent years seeking something outside myself. That every one of the answers had been within me, the entire time. I had wasted years trying to find myself, while declaring I wanted *to find my family,* when my adopted family was my family. A family I could have enjoyed so much more, if I had only realized the gifts of experience they added to my personal journey.

I began to feel very connected to my ancestors—both biological and adopted. I hope you will have a similar experience of discovering and engaging the ancestors that are within you, and that your questions will lead you to answers. In the Introduction, you'll find some techniques to help you make the most of the prompts to discover more and better information.

These 52 exercises, created by our expert authors will allow you to reach out to your ancestors, whether you know who they are or not. Even if you know of them and don't care much for some of their traits or behaviors, you can use this journal to understand them in new ways. Here, you get 52 experiences, discovering and embracing the ancestral aspects of your family members—characteristics that live on within you.

Your ancestors have waited your whole life for THIS moment!

...and your next!

The Ancestors Within Journal

works beautifully alongside

- *The Ancestors Within, Volume I: Reveal and Heal the Ancient Memories You Carry*
- *The Ancestors Within, Volume 2: Discover & Connect with Your Ancient Origins*

Purchase *The Ancestors Within* on Amazon and Kindle!

Join us on Facebook!

Would you like to meet the authors and learn more about their insights and perspectives? Would you like to be first to know about next volume of *The Ancestors Within* and new ways to discover more amazing ancestral connections? Join us today on The Ancestors Within Community Facebook group. https://www.facebook.com/groups/ancestorswithin

CONTENTS

INTRODUCTION

Before you dive into the following pages, I'd like you to consider using this journal in a whole new way. Obviously, it can be a private journal (as most journals are), but it has the potential to be created as a family heirloom, a journal of your experiences discovering and connecting with your ancestors. Imagine a beloved great-grandchild finding this book and reading of your experiences connecting with your own great-grandparents. Your great-grandchild would be reading about ancestors *six generations* in their past.

The journal is organized into 52 numbered weeks (though you can, of course, use the prompts in any order you choose). Each week offers information or ideas for you to contemplate, along with a few lined pages for your response. Most weeks include closing comments or a blessing, and all of them include information about the prompt's author. Many authors include quotes from *The Ancestors Within* that will add to your insight.

The quotes and ideas in the journal closely connect with *The Ancestors Within* (Volumes 1 and 2), making this a companion journal. In fact, one way to use this journal is to sit down with *The Ancestors Within,* complete a chapter in that book, and then journal your experience here in the companion guide. If you use this process, you will notice there are six bonus chapters in the journal. These are also indicated in the authors byline; for example, "Week Eleven: The Spring Equinox, "Bonus Chapter by Dr. Ahriana Platten."

Whether you use the journal alongside the previous books or not, the chapter authors hope you will try several journaling techniques to see what works best for you.

Standard Journaling: Contemplate the prompt (or part of the prompt). Then write what you felt, thought, or experienced during your contemplation. Following Sondra Lambert's guidance in Week Five, for example, you would plant a family tree during the week; then you would write about your experience. Maybe, while planting the tree, you felt drawn toward a certain ancestor. Or maybe you found a coin nearby (or another object), prompting questions: *What year is the coin? What did you feel when you found it?* Stay open to insights and connections revealed through details.

Sometimes, while writing, you may need more space. For example, you might want to try all of the journaling methods in this list for each prompt—automatic writing on Monday, dreamwork on Tuesday, and so on. Or you may want to respond to each bullet point in one of the more expansive prompts. In these instances, you can obviously record your thoughts elsewhere. Later (especially if you are creating a family keepsake), you can transcribe into the journal your favorite or most insightful results.

Automatic Writing/Channeling: Provide yourself with soft lighting and get comfortable. Hold a pen or pencil loosely in your hand, and bring a question to mind. It can be an exact bullet point or question from the journal prompt, or it can be a question of your own, prompted by what you read. Drawing from Week One, for example, you might begin your contemplation with "Tell me the great clues of my life…" Whatever comes into your mind, write it down as quickly as it comes. Channeling is much like writing a song's lyrics as you listen or like taking dictation—you'll be going too fast to read what you're writing… until you are done.

Dreamwork: Prepare before you go to bed by placing writing supplies and a soft light within reach. As you settle down, ask your ancestors to show you what you are meant to know about a subject, such as (from Week Twenty-Two) "For what purpose did I come to this life?" Be sure to add the request, "Wake me to remember." When you awaken don't move. Don't move. Lie in the same position and ask yourself, *Was I dreaming? What was I dreaming?* For each sliver of memory from your dream, work to remember more by asking yourself questions; for example, *Who was I talking to? What were they wearing? What was I wearing?* Bring as many details as possible to your conscious mind before you move to begin writing.

Sensory Experience: Use this technique when the prompt offers a physical or sensory activity. Write what you felt, heard, smelled, and so on. Working again with The Family Tree (Week 5) you would write about your sensory experience. Perhaps you had a sense of déjà vu, even though you have never planted anything, or maybe you felt cold, even though the day was hot. Perhaps you heard music or someone's voice. Maybe you smelled perfume, though nobody was wearing it, or smelled cigar smoke, though nobody was smoking.

Artistic Journaling/Heart-Mapping: With artistic journaling (which is also called "heart-mapping"), you don't necessarily write words; instead, you draw symbols, people, images, hearts—whatever comes to your mind as you contemplate the prompt. For example, in Week Seven, Jacqueline Kane prompts you to consider, "What's the common health complaint that I hear in my family?" You may find yourself drawing stick figures and circling a spot on the body, such as the heart or a hand. Don't edit… keep drawing! At the end, you can make notes on the page that relate to the drawings. Artistic journaling is a great way to access information your subconscious knows but your conscious mind may not realize.

Guided/Shamanic Journey: This method is a lot like visualization. In week 19, Arielle writes, "We needn't be a certain way to receive words from our ancestors." Let this idea free you to ask whatever you're wondering about—simply relax, ask your question, and visualize, allowing your question to guide you. For example, you might ask, "How do you currently show up in my life?" In contemplation, you might see yourself entering a garden. If so, notice details, and ask questions: Is there a place to sit down? Are there animals, insects, or birds around you? What do you smell? What do you hear? What season is it? As you ask questions, allow the information to come to you. When you feel finished, be sure to thank your ancestors.

Family Journaling: You might choose to complete this journal as a family activity. If so, you could share the week's prompt with the family and have everyone contemplate it as the week goes on. Then each family member can share their favorite or most vivid result. Another way to journal as a family would be for each family member to choose and respond to a different prompt. With either family journaling method, you can have everybody sign and date their special contributions to the journal.

As you reach out to your ancestors, keep in mind you may be creating a family heirloom to be handed down as lovingly as a family photo album or scrap book. Imagine yourself filling a sacred treasure chest with stories of ancestral connection. See, in your mind's eye, future generations of your family opening the treasure chest and finding the gems you are about to create. All of the journal authors wish you the very best experiences connecting with previous generations of your family, and through this journal, future generations as well.

WEEK ONE

THE ADOPTEE'S DREAM

by Amy Gillespie Dougherty

Your ancestors have waited your whole life for THIS Moment! This is even more true if you are adopted or felt blocked from your ancestral information. The true essence of your ancestry lives safe and secure inside of you. YOU are the treasure chest.

As you begin this yearlong exploration, consider the clues that already exist in your experience. Settle into comfort. Breathe easy and request insight and support from your "ancestors within."

Tell me the great clues of my life…

- Unique, bizarre, or even traumatic experiences
- Things that happen over and over to you
- Things you say – quirks and quirky behaviors
- Things you *love* – cultures, hobbies, events in history
- Clothes, personal style (What calls to you?)

____

____

____

____

"I wondered what it would be like to sit down to dinner, surrounded by those who looked like me, laughed like me, felt insecure like me."
– *The Ancestors Within, Vol 1,* p. 1

"Even if you're an identical twin, you are the only person connected to your specific ancestors." – *The Ancestors Within, Vol 1,* p. 1

"You know what you were told about your birth, and that's a clue."
– *The Ancestors Within, Vol. 1,* p. 5

As you close out this week's exploration, express your gratitude for the help you've received: *Thank you for each gift you have brought to me. I wish you love, light and blessings for all that you have been and brought to my life. Thank you for the amazing gifts and experiences you have brought to my life. I can only imagine your greatest joys, fears, frustrations, and even anger at the experiences that happened during your life. I honor you for all that you have experienced.*

"Your ancestors have waited your whole life for THIS moment!"
– *The Ancestors Within, Vol. 1,* p. 1

Amy Gillespie Dougherty, is the founder of *Irigenics*® Ancestral Eye Reading and the non-profit, CLARA (Children's Lives Are the Responsibility of All). She is a results-driven innovator, speaker, and bestselling author with more than twenty years' experience creating impactful self-discovery, awareness, and life-coaching programs. Get access to Amy's tool from *The Ancestors Within* on her website, www.amygillespie.com/resources. Or find Amy on the "Irigenics" YouTube channel.

WEEK TWO

THE SECRETS OF THE STONES

How to Channel Your Ancestors Through Crystals

by Melissa Jolly Graves

> The title of this week's prompt is from Melissa's chapter in *The Ancestors Within, Vol 1.* If you would like to know more about her experiences with stones and crystals, please consult that chapter.

Knowledge obtained with the mind is memory. Knowledge obtained through the heart is wisdom. Seek wisdom through your heart, and you will find the treasures your ancestors have sown within your consciousness.

Write down your problems. Be real with your emotions. Then ask your ancestors to help you find the wisdom needed to heal not only you, but all those around you and those connected to you. Remember, when you live with your heart, you build new opportunities of hope not only for the past, but for the future. Journal the messages that came to you during this experience.

____

____

____

____

____

____

"Remember, knowledge is just knowledge if kept to yourself. We can only obtain wisdom when knowledge is shared."
– *The Ancestors Within, Vol 1,* p. 18

"All willing to listen to the ancestors will learn. All who fully trust will be trusted." – *The Ancestors Within, Vol 1,* p. 16

The ancestors work in many ways, using stones, trees, people's words, the wind, and even the thoughts in your head. You are never alone in life or in death. There are always advisors willing to love you and guide you through any situation. If ever there is a problem you cannot solve, seek the perspectives of your ancestors and guides by listening with your heart.

Melissa Jolly Graves is an exceptional seer, who strives to offer people a new perspective on life. Her accomplishments include being a successful wife and mother, as well as the owner of Euphoric Source. As a teacher, counselor, minister, author, public speaker, and documentarian, Melissa opens the hearts and minds of many. Learn more at www.euphoricsource.com.

WEEK THREE

BRIDGING THE WORLDS

by Asherah Allen

When a loved one passes, we can be left with unspoken words still in our heart. I invite you to take a moment to write a letter to a departed loved one, expressing any sentiments you wish you could have communicated while they were still alive. When you are done, take a moment to conjure the person before you, as you knew him or her in life, maybe making an offering of a favorite food. Then read your letter aloud, trusting that the spirit of your loved one is receiving your heartfelt words. Take time to listen and see if you can hear your loved one responding.

"Blessed be the ancestors, their legacy, and our hallowing of their memory." – *The Ancestors Within, Vol 1,* p. 27

"May the blood of your ancestors, the cords of connection, your chakra wheels, and their legacy of love be a blessed gateway of reunion whenever you have need." – *The Ancestors Within, Vol 1,* p. 27

Beloved of my heart, I trust we will continue to find ways to communicate because I know a bond such as ours can never be broken or forgotten. Thank you for all that you have given to me and for all that we have shared. I give my thanks. Let our union remain, as we now enjoy different means of connecting. Blessed are we who grieve deeply, for so too are we who love deeply.

Asherah Allen is a Certified Spiritual Counselor, grief specialist, and master healer. She is passionately in service to helping people live their most soul-aligned, spiritually infused, radiantly healthy life. Asherah maintains a successful, private in-person and online healing arts practice. Her specialties include trauma integration and pain management. Learn more at www.awakenedhearthealingarts.com. Get access to Asherah's tool from *The Ancestors Within* at www.awakenedhearthealingarts.com/resources.

WEEK FOUR

ANCESTORS AND AUTISM

by Noah Smith

I am autistic and nonverbal, so my ancestral experiences might be very different from yours. I've always heard voices. Now I understand they are ancestors trying to help and guide us. My message is this: Always trust your thoughts when they do not feel like they are yours.

Think of a time when you had a thought that did not feel like your own. What was the thought? Your thoughts that come from someone else are coming from your spirit guides. Journal about these experiences.

Keep writing about the voices in your mind that don't feel like you. Ask who they are and what they have come to teach you. Journal your experience with these ancestral voices and ideas.

____

____

____

____

____

____

____

____

"Know that there are people who can sense, feel, and hear things that you do not." – *The Ancestors Within, Vol 1,* p. 33

"Autism is not a disability but a difference in sensory perception."
– *The Ancestors Within, Vol 1,* p. 33

"Know that I feel energy all the time, so writing this out helps my body focus a bit better." – *The Ancestors Within, Vol 1,* p. 31

Feelings are good but sometimes difficult to express in words. Give yourself time to really remember and experience the telepathic connection with your ancestors.

I hope to hear from new friends. Please reach out to me if you feel moved to learn more.

Noah Smith is known as the "spiritual electrician," sending energy through the soles of the feet. He is a gentle healer whose main goal is to help and serve those in spiritual entanglement and bring them to spiritual enlightenment. Whether he is healing or sending his mother Sharon the message to give you, he will help you relax and bring your energy back to balance. Learn more at www.awakenedhearthealingarts.com or www.sharonsweb.com.

WEEK FIVE

PLANTING A FAMILY TREE

Digging Through the Past and Preserving It for the Future

by Sondra Lambert

This week, plant a family tree. You can do this alone or with other family members. You can even plant the tree in a pot. However you create this experience, pay attention—not just to your physical experience, but to the vibrations you sense and to seemingly insignificant details. As you work, contemplate your family backward and forward through time.

When we are born, we partner with all those who have come before us and all those who will follow in our footsteps. The powerful presence at this moment is significant. Absorb the love, absorb the light, absorb the moment. It is precious. As I have walked my path into the footsteps of my grandfather's grandfathers, I know they believed in everyone who would follow.

Journal of your experience planting a family tree.

____

____

____

____

____

"As I have walked my path into the footsteps of my grandfather's grandfathers, I know they believed in everyone who would follow."
– *The Ancestors Within,* Vol 1, p. 36

"When we are born, we partner with all those who have come before us and all those who will follow in our footsteps."
– *The Ancestors Within, Vol 1,* p. 37

"The powerful presence at this moment is significant. Absorb the love, absorb the light, absorb the moment. It is precious."
– *The Ancestors Within, Vol 1,* p. 44

The lives we live and the ground we stand upon are sacred. Our legacy is gifted to us by those who stood the ground before us. Right or wrong, good or bad, they created the path. We walk in their footsteps. For that gift we say, *Thank you.*

Keep it simple and have fun!

Sondra Lambert is a professional encourager and is very good at her job. For those who seek refreshment, she is a cool glass of water. Drink it in. Learn more at www.galaxyhypnosis.com/Sondra.

WEEK SIX

HEARING MY GRANDMOTHER

How to Use Affirmations to Bridge Communication with Your Ancestors

by Lisa Newton

To learn the wisdom of your ancestors, first build a bridge of communication using meditation and the positive light of affirmations. Affirmations have been universally utilized by spiritually connected people throughout time. Affirmations and meditation have great power to positively guide you on your path.

What is an affirmation that will support you in understanding ancestral connections and energies? What can you write about, right now, that illustrates the ways in which affirmation and meditation have guided you on your path? Perhaps you will hear *your* grandmother in your affirmations or during your meditation.

____

____

____

____

____

____

"To learn the wisdom of your ancestors, first build a bridge of communication using mediation and the positive light of affirmations."
– *The Ancestors Within, Vol 1,* p. 45

"Affirmations have been universally utilized
by spiritually connected people throughout time."
– *The Ancestors Within, Vol 1,* p. 46

"I believe that infants come into the world with all these gifts, and they are silenced by events, societal norms, and life trauma."
– *The Ancestors Within, Vol 1,* p. 52

I believe that infants come into the world with many gifts that are then silenced by events, societal norms, and life trauma. I challenge you, the reader, to regain your gifts and promote them in your children. Have you regained your silent gifts?

Lisa A. Newton, M.Ed. is a lifelong special education and ESL (English as a second language) teacher. She uses her gifts as an intuitive and empath to fulfill her calling as a teacher. She believes that all people have gifts and spiritual powers that they just need to learn how to tap into them, and the key is the use of positive affirmations, learning from elders, and meditation journeying. Learn more at www.earthaffirmations.com.

WEEK SEVEN

UNLOCK YOUR ANCESTRAL STORY

Take Charge of YOUR Life

by Jacqueline Kane

What is "ancestral energy"? I define it as our ancestors' unresolved emotional issues caused by situations or events which were painful or traumatic—such as illnesses, accidents, financial troubles, broken relationships, and so on—any "emotional baggage" that was unsettled, pushed aside, or simply not talked about in their lifetime. Work with your ancestral energy by asking yourself, "What's the common health complaint that I hear in my family?" Record these patterns. Then ask your ancestors how you can help heal these patterns.

"I learned I could turn my pattern of disappointment into excitement to create unlimited possibility."
– *The Ancestors Within, Vol 1,* p. 66

“Ancestral energy is our ancestors’ unresolved emotional issues from situations or events that caused hurt, pain, or trauma and were passed down to us.” – *The Ancestors Within, Vol 1,* p. 66

"The price of not healing this ancestral energy is not standing in your power, crippling self-doubt, confusion, lack of clarity, and lack of action towards your soul's purpose." – *The Ancestors Within, Vol 1,* p. 67

Embrace the new you. Decide what new energy you would love to bring into your body, for example, unconditional love, compassion, or excitement. Bring this new energy into your body and allow this new energy to expand into your entire body. Decide today and claim that this is the new you and that you get to have all that you desire. This is a powerful process that will positively impact all areas of your life.

Jacqueline Kane is an energetic alignment strategist who supports women in discovering the crucial hidden links between their physical pain and their ability to live a full life. With over 30 years in health care, Jacqueline has merged her innate wisdom with a multitude of healing modalities to create a results-oriented method of healing. Learn more at www.jacquelinemkane.com.

WEEK EIGHT

THE WHISPERS OF YOUR ANCESTORS

Connect and Embrace the Power of Your Gifts and Talents

by Deena Chester

This is the week to tap into the ancestral wisdom as it relates to your gifts, talents, and mysteries. Journaling and self-hypnosis are my favorite tools to connect with my ancestral wisdom. Both of these techniques will allow you to bypass the critical, conscious thought processes and drop into the powerful subconscious mind.

Here are some prompts for your journaling this week. Choose a focus. Enter the experience with your senses: sights, smells, tastes, sounds, and feelings. Then set your intention to connect and allow the flow.

- Are there negative or destructive cycles in my life? Are they really mine, or are they from my ancestors or a past life? How can I stop the cycles? Is there a past life that could empower me now?
- Today I will write about what makes my heart sing and ask the ancestors for guidance.

Dear ancestors, thank you for your experiences, gifts, and talents. Please tell me how I can embrace my gifts and talents.

Take a deep breath. Write about your feelings. Let them flow.

"Who is with me? My earth family, like butterflies, bees, rabbits, wolves, deer, skunks, dragons, fairies, wind, moon, and sun."
– *The Ancestors Within, Vol 1,* p. 74

"*Someday I will help and heal others.* This is the message from my grandmothers." – *The Ancestors Within, Vol 1,* p. 74

Blessings and peace to you on your journey. Take the time to explore and hear the subtle messages of your ancestors and your soul.

Deena Chester is an expert healer and owner of Accept Your Power. She is a bestselling author, certified hypnotherapist, past life regression specialist, ancestral eye reader, certified transformational life coach, Reiki Master, and EFT practitioner. She provides intuitive, transformational guidance for spiritual connection, past lives, and your unique life purpose. Deena's powerful blend of modalities will help you live the life you were born to live. She offers individual sessions and workshops, both online and by phone. Learn more at Deena's website, www.acceptyourpower.com. Email Deena at Deena@acceptyourpower.com, or find Deena on social media: "Accept Your Power" on Facebook and deena.chester on Instagram.

WEEK NINE

RAPTURE JOURNALING

Surviving Your Ancestral Story: Recognizing the Opportunity for Change

by Carol Dutton

As you explore your ancestral connections, I invite you to use my RAPTURE Journaling exercise to give thanks to the ancestors and their influences on your life.

R: Recognize a repeating pattern in your life, such as always losing things.
A: Acknowledge how the pattern may have developed in the lives of your ancestor(s). Did they emigrate to a new country? Is the pattern helping you, or is it a hindrance?
P: Praise your ancestors for enduring the struggles that led to the creation of the pattern.
T: Thank your ancestors for their caring. They passed this pattern to you because they thought it would help you. Again, use loving words.
U: Understand how the repeating pattern is and is not serving you in your efforts to live your best life.
R: Release the pattern for your ancestors and yourself. Consider using this affirmation: "I release this pattern from my life, from the lives of my ancestors, and from the lives of all others affected by it."
E: Express and Envision. Express your love to your ancestors for their impact on their world, their descendants, and the universe—and especially their impact on you. Envision your new life with patterns that enhance your ability to live your best life.

Journal how you expressed your love and the vision you have for your life.

____

____

____

"Muscles are connective tissue, so what are the connections within his family ancestry?" – *The Ancestors Within, Vol 1,* p. 85

"They must have shared similar life events that they wanted to connect to him as a way of protection!" – *The Ancestors Within, Vol 1,* p. 86

It is with gratitude to all our ancestors that I share this journaling exercise with you. Their life experiences created the epigenetics that we carry in our current lives. Blessings and love to all the ancestors for all that they endured.

Carol Dutton is the owner of Being You Energetically, LLC, and an expert subtle energy practitioner, Reiki Master, and Irigenics® Ancestral Eye Reading consultant. Her powerful sessions will immediately give you the unique and specific missing links to clearing the traumatic and ancestral patterns keeping you from living an extraordinary life.

WEEK TEN

SHAMANIC JOURNEYING

Breaking Limiting Patterns by Connecting with Our Ancestral Guides

by Tanya L. Colucci

I invite you to light a candle, take a few deep breaths, and bring your awareness into your heart space. Feel into the space of inviting your ancestors and guides to assist you in unraveling some patterns. Take a few moments to write down bullet points—situations, people, scenarios, and events that you need to offer forgiveness.

Then make a second list. Take a few moments to ask yourself what you would like to pull into your life from your heart in order to create that feeling of deliciousness that comes from being more connected with your heart!

____

____

____

____

____

____

____

____

"Use love and forgiveness always, and don't hold onto things."
– *The Ancestors Within, Vol 1,* p. 91

"Do you know that feeling of desire to deeply connect inside, know yourself, heal yourself, serve others, have a deep connection with God/Source, and enjoy life to its fullest with deliciousness?"
– *The Ancestors Within, Vol 1,* p. 92

"Perhaps one step we can take is to unravel those tightly-wound patterns keeping us from experiencing all the multidimensional aspects of ourselves emotionally, physically, energetically, and spiritually."
– *The Ancestors Within, Vol 1,* p. 92-93

Take your first list—the scenarios calling for forgiveness—and write each item on its own small slip of paper. Bringing a small bowl or shell and a lighter, go into nature, asking your guides and ancestors to join you. Take a moment to connect with your heart center. Then begin a fire ceremony, taking great care for safety. Burn each scenario and place it into the bowl or shell to energetically release it for good. Once this process is complete, offer the ashes to Mother Earth.

Tanya Colucci, expert shaman, author, and speaker is the owner of Sacred Soul Guidance and Tanya Colucci Myofascial Release Therapy. Her powerful Sacred Soul Coaching and Healing methods use an extraordinary combination of shamanic work, bodywork, vibrational sound, and ceremonial healing modalities to be your solution for living with joy, purpose, and passion. Learn more at www.sacredsoulguidance.com. Get access to Tanya's tool from *The Ancestors Within* at www.sacredsoulguidance.com/resources.

WEEK ELEVEN

SPRING EQUINOX

Bonus Chapter
by Dr. Ahriana Platten

Spring is here, and like sap, our creative juices begin to flow! Our ancestors are the creative foundation of life. Our minds are filled with ideas that seem new, yet emerge from their experiences and insights. As winter gives way to spring, what new ideas are seedlings in your heart? What will you dig out from the creative closets of your mind and offer to the energy of the sun? How will you carry forward into manifestation the hopes and dreams of those upon whose shoulders you stand?

"The ancestors in my bones awakened."
– *The Ancestors Within, Vol 1,* p. 136

"When I made that promise to my father, I could feel something inside of me spring to life!" – *The Ancestors Within, Vol 1,* p. 135

"I knew her, somehow, and could feel her watching over me."
– *The Ancestors Within, Vol 1,* p. 134

____

____

____

____

____

____

____

____

____

____

____

____

____

____

____

____

May the hopes and dreams of your ancestors flow easily through you. May their wisdom fill your heart and mind — and may all that you create honor their memory and bring them peace.

———

Dr. Ahriana Platten is an international speaker, author, and courage builder. She helps people find their purpose and live into it. She's a master ceremonialist and practical mystic, widely appreciated for her authenticity, her professional insights, and her coaching on the process of change. Find more from Ahriana at www.asoulfullworld.com.

WEEK TWELVE

THE WOVEN WEB

Discovering and Removing Energy Strings

by Marcia Colver Reichert

Have a seat in your favorite chair or couch and ponder for a moment.

What does the web of energy look like? Think of an ancestor you would like to heal your relationship with. What does the filament that connects you look like? What colors do you see? Then consider the threads that connect you with all those you care for. Are they all the same color, or do some look different because of different or unhealed relationships? Do you see the strands between you and an ancestor that are cloudy or mucked up in any way? Is there anything you can do to make the strings become more clear and bright?

____

____

____

____

____

____

____

____

"You need to live in the real world and get out of your head!"
– *The Ancestors Within, Vol 1,* p. 101

"The trauma is like the filaments that make up a web, weaving throughout multiple lifetimes or generations." – *The Ancestors Within, Vol 1,* p. 104

"If you can imagine that all of those strings that connect us have power as energy, perhaps you can imagine that we could clear those energy strings so that hate and resentment were cleared and love and appreciation remained."
– *The Ancestors Within, Vol 1,* p. 104

Give thanks to your ancestors for the insights you've gained.

Thank you so much for connecting with me and showing me the energy between us, that connects us. Bless you for being open to helping me clear that connection and making it stronger with love. Thank you for helping me clear other connections and showing me ways to improve my life. May you forever remain in love and peace.

Marcia Colver Reichert began life with amazing abilities and perspectives. She travels to spread joy, wonder, and healing to people throughout the world. She is a best-selling author, mentor, shaman, master of healing arts, High Priestess and alchemist. Her goal is to help you "Step Into Your Magic." Learn more at www.marciacolver.com. Find Marcia's tool from *The Ancestors Within* at marciacolver.com/ancestors-within-book.

WEEK THIRTEEN

THE HEART SPACE

The Portal to Ancestral Healing

by Michelle Troupe

We all have a story. What if your story has a beginning beyond your wildest dreams? You are more than this lifetime. You are a soul who is connected to many ancestors. Open your heart to all that is you, and connect with your ancestors. Journal about the beginning of your story—the very beginning, back through generations. It is time to know the truth of who you are from the deepest, open space in your heart.

"For me, the unknown became more about trusting and enjoying the journey." – *The Ancestors Within, Vol 1,* p. 111

"It allowed me to dig deeper without fear
and get closer to knowing who I am."
– *The Ancestors Within, Vol 1,* p. 111

"With understanding, there is no judgment of self or others."
– *The Ancestors Within, Vol 1,* p. 113

Connect with your heart space (the seed of your soul) on a daily basis as you awake in the morning and before you go to bed. Express gratitude for all parts of you, your ancestors, and the day. Embrace the unknown and the willingness to expand beyond your wildest dreams.

Michelle Troupe is a Quantum Lightworker, Integrated Energy Therapy® Master Teacher, and Certified Sound Healer. Michelle has a unique ability to awaken you to the light within and to open your heart to the truth of who you are. Her work is a catalyst to shifting into higher levels of consciousness. Learn more at her website, www.earthangelhealingllc.com. Get access to Michelle's tool from *The Ancestors Within* at www.earthangelhealingllc.com/resources-to-assist-you-on-your-path.

WEEK FOURTEEN

RECONNECTING THE BROKEN BONDS AND HONORING OUR ANCESTORS

Life-Changing Healing Practices

by Phoenix Trueblood

From birth, we are given an amazing gift, the gift of life. This gift comes from our ancestors and is a connection to our soul. We are its caretakers, and then it becomes our gift to future generations. I invite you to ask your ancestors: *What is my unique gift? How was I intended to use it? Which of my ancestors had this gift? Please guide me to what is important for me to know about my gift. Please help me stay connected. Show me how to honor you.*

"We are immortal spiritual beings living an only temporary human experience." – *The Ancestors Within, Vol 1*, p. 115

"Never let the chain of kindness go unbroken, and the links of love, compassion, and kind acts will eventually encircle the world."
– *The Ancestors Within, Vol 1,* p. 123

"Are you ready to release yourself and your future generations from past ancestral trauma—the trauma that has you asking yourself, *Why is this happening to me? Why is my life so messed up? Why can't I have the life I want?*"
– *The Ancestors Within, Vol 1,* p. 113

Our ancestors have guided us our entire lives. Let's give thanks to them for helping with this exercise to activate your unlimited potential and your best way to bring it into the world. Close this exercise by writing your intention on paper. Then burn the paper (carefully!) in a container and mix the ashes into a plant that will grow with your ability to access and bring forth your amazing gift. You can also take the extinguished ashes and spread them into the wind with a prayer of gratitude, allowing the universe to accept the ashes, along with your best intentions.

———

Phoenix Trueblood is a gifted shamanic practitioner. Working with earth elements and energies since she was a child, she is the granddaughter of a respected elder and medicine woman who lived until the age of 103. Learn more about Phoenix and her work at phoenixtrueblood.net.

WEEK FIFTEEN

BECOMING A TRANSITIONAL CHARACTER

Leverage Your Ancestral Gifts to Heal Transgenerational Trauma

by Elizabeth R. Kipp

The ancestors may have left their karmic residue for us to clean up, but their infinite nature endures beyond the bounds of time. Ancestral Clearing® helps us release our stuck energy to no longer regret the past nor try to banish it. When we heal this energy, we heal ourselves, our lineage and the world, thus becoming a transitional character—one who changes the entire course of a lineage.

Our ancestors live in our heartbeat and in every cell of our bodies. The soul knows all about this ancient energy, has always known it, and will forever know it. The wonder of creation expressed through the human heart is the eternal dance of love. It pulsed in all your ancestors, and they passed it on to you.

What is the karmic residue affecting your life? Journal about the ways you might release stuck energy and make peace with the past. How can you heal yourself in order to help heal your lineage and the world?

____

____

____

"The ancestors may have left their karmic residue for us to clean up, but their infinite nature endures beyond the bounds of time."
– *The Ancestors Within, Vol 1,* p. 129

"Ancestral Clearing® helps us release our stuck energy
to no longer regret the past nor banish it."
– *The Ancestors Within, Vol 1,* p. 131

"When we heal ourselves, we heal our lineage and heal the world."
– *The Ancestors Within, Vol 1*, p. 131

We are born with our ancestors' gifts and limitations. It is up to each of us to leverage our strengths, given to us by them, in order to release our common burdens. They gesture in so many ways, encouraging us to remember our place under the stars and to become transitional characters. When we heal ourselves, we heal our lineage and heal the world.

Elizabeth Kipp is a chronic pain specialist, yoga-informed addiction recovery coach, Ancestral Clearing® Practitioner, yoga and meditation teacher, and international best-selling author of *The Way Through Chronic Pain: Tools to Reclaim Your Healing Power*. She focuses on helping people realize the power of their inherent healing at www.elizabeth-kipp.com.

WEEK SIXTEEN

WHEN THE HOMELAND CALLS

by Ahriana Platten

Consider the fact that current science says we carry the epigenetic signature of 11 generations. That's roughly 400 years! As you consider what you know about your ancestors—where they came from and what they lived through—ask yourself, also, what wounds they may have passed to you. Did they live through famine? War? Plague? Natural crises like earthquakes or hurricanes? What difficulties did your ancestors face that might be woven into who you are? What did they fear? What made them strong?

____

____

____

____

____

____

____

____

____

____

____

____

“Their blood runs in our veins. Our bones and skin are formed in their fashion.” – *The Ancestors Within, Vol 1,* p. 133

"We carry their losses in our bodies, hearts, and minds."
– *The Ancestors Within, Vol 1,* p. 134

"Trans-generational wounds are passed down to us, woven into the fabric of our being."
– *The Ancestors Within, Vol 1,* p. 138

May your ancestors find peace through your release of ancestral wounds. May your ancestors send you their strength as you explore what is ready to be released. May you and your ancestors come together in harmonious union to bring forth wisdom and light in the world.

Dr. Ahriana Platten is an international speaker, author, and courage builder. She helps people find their purpose and live into it. She's a master ceremonialist and practical mystic, widely appreciated for her authenticity, her professional insights, and her coaching on the process of change. Find more from Ahriana at www.asoulfullworld.com.

WEEK SEVENTEEN

SINGING FROM ANCESTORS

Bonus Chapter
by Marcia Colver Reichert

Do you remember any elders in your family singing you to sleep? If so, how did that feel? If not, how do you imagine it would feel? Our earth sings for us all the time, as do all the heavenly bodies. Is there an ancestor of a certain heritage that you'd like to connect with? What songs did they sing? As you contemplate these questions, and as you write this week, I encourage you to sing whatever comes to your head because it may hold a message for you. There is always music in our world. Are you willing to slow your mind and hear it? It really is a gift.

Thank you, Spirit, for the gift of music and for allowing me to slow my world enough to experience it. Blessings to all the ancestors who came through to remind me of their songs. Help me feel my soul's song so that I may know I am headed in the correct direction.

Marcia Colver Reichert began life with amazing abilities and perspectives. She travels to spread joy and wonder to the world through her voice. She is a best-selling author, mentor, shaman, master of healing arts, High Priestess, and channel of song. Her goal is to help you "step into your magic." Learn more at www.marciacolver.com. Get access to Marcia's tool from *The Ancestors Within* at www.marciacolver.com/ancestors-within-book.

WEEK EIGHTEEN

BUILDING RELATIONSHIPS WITH YOUR ANCESTORS

Connecting with the Power of Your Ancient Bloodline to Heal Generational Trauma

by Crystal Rasmussen

I invite you to pause for a moment, take a deep breath, close your eyes, and feel the memory of your ancestors pulsing through your veins. Feel their love for you. Feel your ancestors' gifts and strengths, along with the prayers they have for you. No matter what is happening in your life, they are with you. Invite forth their wisdom, support, and protection. Communicate with them. Share with them what is happening in your life, your challenges and your celebrations. Ask them to help you in your daily life and watch what unfolds in your life with their presence.

____

____

____

____

____

____

"Connecting to your ancestors is one of the most supportive and rewarding relationships you will have." – *The Ancestors Within, Vol 1,* p. 153

"Your ancestors are with you every day. They reside in your blood and bones. Their memories are stored in your cells."
– *The Ancestors Within, Vol 1,* p. 154

"You are never alone. We are here with you."
– *The Ancestors Within, Vol 1,* p. 147

At the close of every day, light a candle, ground yourself into the Earth, take three deep, cleansing breaths, and open your heart to your ancestors. Invite them into your sacred space, make an offering to them, and be in deep gratitude for their presence throughout the day. Ask them if there is anything they would like to share with you. Then listen. Before blowing out the candle, thank them for their guidance, love, wisdom, and support.

Crystal Rasmussen, a Generational Healing® Teacher and Spiritual Guide, supports you in releasing pain and suffering from your ancient bloodline stored within your genetic lineage to heal you today. She also teaches women to communicate with their ancestors, awaken their spiritual gifts and heal inherent family trauma as a Generational Healer®. Learn more at her website, www.crystalrasmussen.com.

WEEK NINETEEN

LETTING GO

by Arielle

We needn't be a certain way to receive words from our ancestors. Our ancestors are always reaching out, speaking, flowing love to us. Never do they pull their focus, appreciation, or assistance from us. If we don't hear from them, it is because we have beliefs blocking the way. Be open to ambiguity as they flow support in your direction. There is no limit to the ways they might communicate with you. Allow yourself to feel them; when a message or inkling stands out to you, allow that. Journal your experiences.

"You had to move your beliefs
that I didn't love you enough to come through."
– *The Ancestors Within, Vol 1,* p. 162

"We've been chomping at the bit to assist you."
– *The Ancestors Within, Vol 1,* p. 163

"The many have much to say."
– *The Ancestors Within, Vol 1,* p. 163

As you move forward in days to come, be open to allowing the momentum of your experiences to build. Everyone starts where they are; there is no wrong place to begin. Your ancestors seek a relationship with you. Their assistance and appreciation of you is never-ending. With every step you take in the unique direction of your desires, a new vantage point is born. Enjoy!

Arielle of The Collective Consultation is an enthusiastic interpreter of the vibrational communication of the non-physical. As such, she hosts interactive consultation sessions for clients with the non-physical aspects of those currently living, those previously physical, and the consciousness of infinite intelligence. To learn more, visit Arielle's website at www.thecollectiveconsultation.com.

WEEK TWENTY

ANCESTRAL HEALTH THROUGH GENEALOGY

Find and Recognize Repetitive Family Patterns

by Jeanne Ruczak-Eckman

"You live as long as you are remembered."
~ Russian Proverb

This week, reach out to the elders of your family. Story-time is not just for kids! Ask them about repetitive family patterns that might need healing.

- Write a letter – an actual letter – to an elder of your family.
- Remember the pleasantries.
- Ask no more than three specific questions about your ancestors.
- Ask questions about someone they should know well.
- Remember to thank them.

"Stories are what make one's family tree interesting."
– *The Ancestors Within, Vol 1,* p. 165

"Forgiveness. That was my first lesson in ancestral healing."
– *The Ancestors Within, Vol 1,* p. 169

“Ancestral healing is a process—a spiritual, ritualistic process—in which we work with our ancestors to recognize, understand, and heal the issue passed through the generations, consciously or unconsciously.”
– *The Ancestors Within, Vol 1,* p. 169

Please remember, some stories are not yours to tell. Others may need to be put into historical context. Your ancestral correspondence is not the place for dirty laundry. May your ancestors' memory be eternal. Vishnaya Pamyat!

Jeanne Ruczhak-Eckman is a seeker of ancestors, yours and hers. She has been walking this life's passage with her ancestors as long as she can remember. As a resource goddess, she can help you connect to your ancestors and walk your ancestral passage. She offers tips and guides at www.ancestralpassages.com.

WEEK TWENTY-ONE

TURNING CURSES INTO BLESSINGS

by Rika Rivka Markel

I invite you to choose one of your ancestors to work with. Pick someone you feel close with, but who is not with you anymore in this reality. Close your eyes for a few minutes and ask that relative to share something you don't already know, but that would be very helpful to you at this time in your life. Consider, especially, any family "curse" that could be turned into a blessing. Then open your eyes and start writing. Don't think about it. Just write until you feel you are done. Then read it again. You will be surprised by the message that you get. Good luck!

___

___

___

___

___

___

___

___

___

___

___

"We are spiritual beings having a human experience."
– *The Ancestors Within, Vol 1,* p. 178

"Once you conquer whatever it is that they trigger in you, they are liberated too." – *The Ancestors Within, Vol 1,* p. 179

"As long as you give others the power to influence your happiness, victim consciousness is winning." – *The Ancestors Within, Vol 1,* p. 179

Always remember: Our ancestors are so proud of us, no matter what happened in their lifetime. It was all meant to be, one way or another, and it was all meant to help us become more loving and caring human beings.

Rika Rivka Markel is a women's empowerment coach and clearing facilitator who will help you detach from your past and thrive. With 30 years of expertise in holistic tools, strategies, and mindset hacks, she'll help you take responsibility for your life and release the circle of blame and shame. Rika recently became a Proctor Gallagher Consultant. Learn more at www.ancestrygems.com or www.rivkamarkel.com.

WEEK TWENTY-TWO

CLEARING ANCESTRAL TRAUMA

Letting Go of the Cycle of Pain and Trauma

by James Kealiipiilani Kawainui

I believe the soul chooses the physical body it comes into, as well as the people it will be in relationship with. This is done as part of its process of growth and expansion. Before we can look at what we may have inherited from our ancestors, we must first acknowledge that we came into embodiment for the lessons and understanding that allow us to grow toward increased self-awareness and enlightenment.

With this understanding, we can heal ancestral trauma and move forward, independent of old patterns and conditioning, choosing how to live our lives. Invite your ancestors to join the experience. Then work with your ancestors to heal lingering traumas. Take time to journal about these experiences.

With gratitude and love, I invite my ancestors into this healing circle…

"We always wanted you to have our knowledge. We share that freely with you always. It is here for you whenever you need it. It is a part of you. Know that as Truth." – *The Ancestors Within, Vol 1,* p. 184

"What happened to us in our lives is our burden to bear, not yours. We ask that you let all of it go and give it back to us."
– *The Ancestors Within, Vol 1,* p. 185

"Traumatic events affect us so deeply that they can literally change the vibration and frequency of our cellular structure, down to the atomic level and the DNA." – *The Ancestors Within, Vol 1,* p. 185

Beloved family, thank you for being a part of my life. Thank you for the wisdom, the gifts, and the challenges that you freely share with me. I also give thanks to my guides, guardians, and angels for their support through this honoring and this ceremony.

James Kawainui is a Native Hawaiian healer and teacher who is an expert in clearing energetic blockages caused by trauma, injury and illness so people can experience freedom, hope, and clarity in their lives. James' passion and commitment is to help people live positive, productive, pain-free lives. Learn more at www.jameskawainui.com. Get access to James' tool from *The Ancestors Within* at www.jameskawainui.com/givingbackceremony.

WEEK TWENTY-THREE

ANCESTRAL POWER

Claim Your Sacred Wisdom and Magic

by Jen Piceno

Make the following requests to your ancestors and journal your results.

Ancestors, join me in this time and space. Surround me with your love, share with me our ancestral power, show me the magic and wisdom available through our lineage as words pour through me. Teach me what it is you wish me to know and help me understand deeply.

"The cycle of life is ever-expansive."
– *The Ancestors Within, Vol 1,* p. 195

"On the magical quest to self-mastery, we travel with heart-opening intentions that propel us forward with great purpose."
– *The Ancestors Within, Vol 1,* p. 194

"Everything is intertwined with eclectic, worldly wisdom
and delivered with purpose-driven intention."
– *The Ancestors Within, Vol 1,* p. 192

Ancestors, thank you for guiding me back to our family wisdom, magic, and power. This mystical path is filled with divine clues, and I am grateful that you are walking with me each step of the way.

Jen Piceno is a business and spiritual wealth consciousness coach, shaman, priestess, and energy medicine specialist with 30+ years of expertise. Through multi-sensory experiences, ancestral healing, and channeling the divine, she'll help you bust through restrictions so you can begin the transformation you've been craving in any area of your life. Get ready to align with everything you were meant to be in ways you've never experienced before. Learn more at www.jenpicneo.com. Get access to Jen's tool from *The Ancestors Within* at www.jenpicneo.com/resources.

WEEK TWENTY-FOUR

CONNECTING THROUGH HEART

by Jonianne Jeannette

Practice guided imagery each day with the intention of permitting yourself to be in flow with the heart/mind waves. Develop your own attunement to this living energy, noticing your experiences, beginning with "I see, I hear, I feel, I taste, I smell, I know, and I sense." Accept each awareness as true and trustworthy. By day three, you will be in the practice of receiving/connecting to heart and can put forth your request for ancestral connection, known or unknown to you. Journal your experience, enjoying the prompts, such as *Where, When, Who, Why,* and *What.* Close with, *Thank you, until we meet again.*

"The innate observer in me kept me consciously aware that I needed help."
– *The Ancestors Within, Vol 1,* p. 202

"I started to develop an awareness of my giving heart,
my capacity to love, and the awareness of my receiving heart."
– *The Ancestors Within, Vol 1,* p. 204

"That love washes through us in waves and entrains the heart and the mind into the same wavelength is a consciousness connected to universal light and energy. These waves have names like alpha, beta, high beta, delta, theta, and gamma." – *The Ancestors Within, Vol 1*, p. 204

As you close your session, bask in the powerful moment of self-directed love, allowing yourself to take full ownership of your whole spirit. Transition your presence into the current moment, acknowledging your ancestor's whole spirit and willingness to connect with thanks and more love.

Jonianne Jeannette, a mystically inspired Certified Massage Therapist, energy wellness practitioner, and Irigenics® Ancestral Eye Reading consultant offers you a broad toolbox to assist in your connection to self-care, with her number one tool being the energy called love. She can work in person, by distance, or through tutorials she facilitates expanding the teachings of one of her long-time teachers, Cyndi Dale. She is online at www.jonnionthespot.com.

WEEK TWENTY-FIVE

OUR ANCESTORS, THE WAY-SHOWERS

Creating Flow by Making Life-Changing Decisions With Ease

by Myrna Y. Triano

Reach out to your ancestors with a message such as the following. Then journal your results.

My Dearest Ancestor,

Show me the way to my talents, strengths, value, and personal insight. Why do I act a certain way in front of a crowd? Or behind closed doors? How do I surrender to trust? Why am I hesitant to pursue what I love to do, when others seem to think, "It's not right" or "It's not enough"? What keeps me from getting to know you? Help me learn through you, by learning about you. Please show me the way.

With love, Your Descendant

____

____

____

____

____

____

"YOU are heard; YOU are a divine being of eternal light and unconditional love. YOU got this!"
– *The Ancestors Within, Vol 1,* p. 216

"Make your mark in this world. You are valuable. You are a treasure."
– *The Ancestors Within, Vol 1,* p. 215

"Be yourself. Be who you are. That is enough."
– *The Ancestors Within, Vol 1*, p. 213

____

____

____

____

____

____

____

____

____

____

____

____

____

____

I am beyond grateful for discovering your laughter, joys, frustrations, and experiences while getting to know you! As I walk now in your footsteps, I have a better understanding of my uniqueness of self and how little bits of you have been passed down to me. I am thankful to be your descendant. I'm not alone. You and my other ancestors are constantly with me, showing me the way, as you continue to inspire me and guide me.

———

Myrna Y. Triano is a Licensed Massage Therapist, Craniosacral Therapy Practitioner, Master Teacher and Practitioner of Integrated Energy Therapy®. Myrna's mental imagery healing methodology can evaluate the body, karmic, spiritual and to the ethereal. She is a motivator, innovator and is a bridge to your soul's mission. Learn more at www.triangelrivers.com.

WEEK TWENTY-SIX

WORLD WITHIN WORLDS

by Nari Anastarsia

It's wonderful if you're open to the opinions of others, but be discerning. Use your inner knowing to decipher and interpret what feels right for you. Many look for the source of all life outside themselves. But if you truly wish to connect to that greater pool of conscious love, look within. There, you will find the world within the worlds. Inside you, the cosmic universe spans, with inner worlds and stars. Yes. Inside you! This is also where you find your ancestors - go within and ask them, *What is the greatest gift I bring to this world?*

"Peace comes within the sounds of men when they realize their oneness with the universe, when they realize it is really everywhere, it is in each one of us." – Black Elk

"See yourself as the greater body and within you the cell that also needs to hold its vibration and healthy light."

– *The Ancestors Within, Vol 2,* Introduction

You are a creative God of infinite power and light. The more you come to understand this truth, the more you will be amazed by the power you hold as an individual to manifest and bring about peace and change.

Thank you for all you and your ancestors bring to our universe!

As an intuitive soul guide and artist, Nari Anastarsia's love and deep connection to the universe is beautifully and uniquely expressed through her visionary light-filled artworks. Through her creativity, she facilitates healing that touches the soul and awakens the heart. Serving as an inspirational beacon of light, Nari's work quietly illuminates souls from all around the world. Learn more at www.narianastarsia.com.

WEEK TWENTY-SEVEN

THE ANCESTRAL KEY

Unlocking the DVD of Your Ancestors

by Amy Gillespie Dougherty

Today's your day, the day your ancestors have waited for your whole life. Today you discover your ancestors are alive within you: their memories, unresolved traumas, outcries, interests, skills, and abilities. What if I could show you how to play the movie trailer of your life? That experience would provide tantalizing details about the ALL of your existence—your personal genesis and the existence of your ancestors. You could use your own eye photos as an access point.

Wouldn't you like to see the trailer of your movie? Let's give that a try. Visit the "Irigenics" channel on YouTube to learn how to take an awesome eye photo.

If you feel your photos have a bit of blur or you aren't seeing images of your ancestors, just focus on an area and ask it what information it holds for you. Each time you look at your photos you will see more ancestral images.

"Are we looking to discover the greatest *I* that we can become by looking back to the greatest our ancestors have been?"
– *The Ancestors Within, Vol 2,* Introduction

"Could it be possible to dream a dream they (your ancestors) dreamt when they were alive?" – *The Ancestors Within, Vol 2,* Introduction

"What message, gift, or information do you have for me?"
– *The Ancestors Within, Vol 2,* p. 9

Thank you for your time, for the life you've lived, for the hardships you've endured. Thank you for sharing your experience with me. I bless you for all you have been and all you have brought to my life. Thank you.

Amy Gillespie Dougherty, is the founder of Irigenics® Ancestral Eye Reading and the non-profit, CLARA (Children's Lives Are the Responsibility of All). She's a results-driven innovator, speaker, and bestselling author with more than twenty years' experience creating impactful self-discovery, awareness, and life coaching programs. Get access to Amy's tool from *The Ancestors Within* at www.amygillespie.com/resources. Visit the "Irigenics" channel on YouTube to learn how to take an eye photo. For a free journal focused on ancestral eye reading, visit www.irigenics.com/freejournal.

WEEK TWENTY-EIGHT

TOOLS FOR ANCESTRAL CONNECTION

Using Sacred Objects for More Clarity

by Lisa A. Newton

Traditional ancestral altars may have a picture display, along with bowls of fresh fruit, herbs, or other offerings. They are designed to invite the ancestor to remain active in the family. Modern ancestral altars are tended to by attention and careful dusting. Like traditional altars, modern altars are given a prominent place in the home. How do you honor your ancestors? What do your modern altars look like?

How will you know a sacred object for your ancestral altar when you see it? You feel it in your intuition, in your gut, or you feel an irrational desire to protect it, even though it may have little monetary value. Describe the sacred objects in your possession and to how they connect you to your biological or adopted ancestor(s). Reflect on your ancestral altars.

"I advocate for creating an ancestral altar for people you hold sacred and honor that are not blood relatives. For example, my [adopted] daughter's ancestor is her grandfather, my dad. Bloodline has little to do with it."
– *The Ancestors Within, Vol 2,* p. 12

"The altar is an antique dining sideboard that already holds the military flag and pictures of other generations. This may not be what initially comes to mind when thinking about sacred objects and ancestral altars."
– *The Ancestors Within, Vol 2,* p. 12

Lisa A. Newton, M.Ed. is a lifelong special education and English as a second language educator. She has developed three virtual language arts curriculums and currently teaches in a public school system. She uses her gifts as an intuitive and empath to fulfill her calling as a teacher. She believes that all people have gifts and spiritual powers that they just need to learn how to tap into them, and the key is the use of positive affirmations, learning from elders, and meditation journeying. Learn more at www.earthaffirmations.com.

WEEK TWENTY-NINE

YOUR MISSING LINK

Healing for Flawed, Forgotten, or Outcast Ancestors

by Joy Andreasen

This week, think about your ancestors, especially any "missing links," such as those who were absent or who lived an unwell life. Perhaps you chose to cut someone out of your life due to toxic behavior, or perhaps someone chose to be absent, for reasons known or unknown to you. This week, write a letter to a missing ancestor. Get it all out on paper. Your anger, your grief, your loss, or your longing for their presence. Think about what beliefs you have that may stem from their absence or presence in your life.

"Your Missing Link Healing For Flawed, Forgotten or Outcast Ancestors."
– *The Ancestors Within, Vol 2,* Chapter 3

"Most of us live our lives completely oblivious to the beliefs that unconsciously drive us." – *The Ancestors Within, Vol 2,* p. 19

"How can we acknowledge ancestors who may have had their very existence erased, hidden, or stashed away somewhere?"
– *The Ancestors Within, Vol 2,* p. 12

After you have spoken your truth, release it all. Forgive the ancestor if necessary, or at least be willing to forgive. Ask the ancestor for their blessing and ask that they be blessed in the journey of their soul. Ask for healing to come to both of you, for example: *Dear Ancestor: I thank you for the gift of life. I forgive you for your mistakes. Please forgive me for mine. May we both be blessed.*

"You may choose to write down what you want to say to the ancestor. You will be reading it or saying it out loud to them."
– *The Ancestors Within, Vol 2,* p. 24

Joy Andreasen is an author, psychic, medium, and Shamanic Reiki Energy Healer. With over twenty years of experience delivering messages from the world of Spirit and facilitating healing of the soul, she sees clients and hosts spiritual gatherings via Zoom, phone, and face-to-face in her office in Winchester Virginia. To learn more, visit her website, www.whispersofjoy.net. Get access to the tool Joy created for *The Ancestors Within* at www.whispersofjoy.net/single-post/honoring-our-ancestors.

WEEK THIRTY

YOUR ARCHETYPES, YOUR ANCESTORS, AND YOUR INNER CHILD

You Are the Medicine and the Method That You Seek

by Dana Louise Williams

When we have unhealed, deeply buried childhood wounds, the time will come when those wounds are uncovered, awakened, and activated. We are designed to recreate whatever we haven't healed from childhood, and we'll unconsciously recreate unhealed wounds through our adult relationships, our health, our money, and our career.

When we heal our childhood wounds, we also heal damaged epigenetic patterns and shift the archetypes within our ancestral lineage. We can also uncover and awaken our own buried gifts, creating a new healing highway for our ancestors and future generations. I invite you to ask your ancestors:

What is important for me to uncover and heal at this time?

____

____

____

____

____

____

____

"The creative spirit needs to have its way with us."
– *The Ancestors Within, Vol 2,* p. 28

"Even back then, as a seer and a visionary, I knew certain truths that I couldn't necessarily express or explain."
– *The Ancestors Within, Vol 2,* p. 29

"My favorite quote from St. Francis is beautifully applied here:
What you are looking for is looking for you."
– *The Ancestors Within, Vol 2,* p. 32

I hope you found healing through this journaling activity. I wish for you a life filled with love, healing, and many blessings. I wish this for you and for the ancestors who live on within you.

Dana Louise Williams, Soul Mission Mentor and Artist of Change, is an EFT/NLP intuitive Coach, Certified Hypnotherapist, Eden Energy Medicine Practitioner, Akashic Records Ancestral Healing Practitioner, and Creator of The Soular Healing Method®. She uses her many years' worth of her own channeled metaphoric drawings when working with clients. Learn more at www.danalouisewilliams.com. Get access to Dana's tool from *The Ancestors Within* at www.danalouisewilliams.com/ancestors2bookbonuses.

WEEK THIRTY-ONE

ANCESTRAL FAMILY HEALING

Clearing Past Pain for a Brilliant Future

by Ariann Thomas

Our ancestors bequeathed us our genes, beliefs, and heritage. Ancestors come from multiple backgrounds of wealth, poverty, power, enslavement, happiness, and desperation. They have a broad perspective of wisdom they are eager and willing to share.

Often families carry unresolved burdens from the past that were not cleared before the ancestor crossed over. Issues such as poverty, pain from illnesses, and relationship difficulties may continue, in repeating patterns, through multiple generations. If we encounter such challenges in our life and need advice, our ancestors are there to help. They want to see us happy and successful.

Are you carrying unresolved burdens? What are they? Ask your ancestors for help healing these old wounds and setting down these burdens.

____

____

____

____

____

"We can all connect with our ancestors for love, support, and help when we need it." – *The Ancestors Within, Vol 2,* p. 40

"Your ancestors are there to help you."
– *The Ancestors Within, Vol 2,* p. 40

"Your ancestors love you and have a great perspective on life that they are delighted to share when asked." – *The Ancestors Within, Vol 2,* p. 44

Ancestor, thank you for guiding me to this healing and clearing of this challenge and belief. Thank you for changing your life and creating a new energy pattern for me and all your descendants to carry into the future. Permanently set this new energy into my genes and energy field to bring happiness and success to me and my family. And So It Is!

Ariann Thomas is an author, international healer, teacher, ceremonialist, speaker, Shaman and Akashic Record Reader. She carries the ancient wisdom and subtle energy of an elder and advisor. Ariann is part Cherokee by heritage. She is the author of *Healing Family Patterns* (2012) and *Changing Our Genetic Heritage* (2018). Learn more at www.ancestrallineageclearing.com.

WEEK THIRTY-TWO

CONNECTING WITH OUR ORIGINAL ANCESTORS

Bonus Chapter
by Joy Andreasen

Have you ever considered the truth that our lives spring from the dirt under our feet and the dust of the stars? Mother Earth and Father Sky are our original ancestors.

Ancient peoples discovered wisdom and truth by tuning in to their natural environment. We, too, can receive messages and guidance from connecting with aspects of nature. Try this. Sit in silence, in a natural environment if possible. Close your eyes.

After you have centered yourself, choose something in nature, such as the sun, the moon, a bird, or a tree and imagine merging with it or having a conversation with it. If it could speak, what would it say? Tell it your secrets and ask for guidance. For the next few days, tune in to nature and see what wisdom she wants to share. Journal the result.

Blessing to our original ancestors:

Dear Mother Earth and Father Sky: Thank you for my life. Thank you for allowing me to live and breathe, to laugh and cry. Every blessing I have comes from you. I will try to live my life realizing the truth of our interconnectedness. Thank you for every moment. Bless you.

Joy Andreasen is an author, psychic, medium, and Shamanic Reiki Energy Healer. With over twenty years' experience delivering messages from the world of spirit and facilitating healing of the soul, she sees clients and hosts spiritual gatherings via Zoom, phone, and face-to-face in her office in Winchester Virginia. Learn more at www.whispersofjoy.net. Get access to Joy's tool from *The Ancestors Within* at www.whispersofjoy.net/single-post/finding-our-purpose-in-life.

WEEK THIRTY-THREE

THE SONG OF YOUR SOUL

Remembering and Healing Spiritual Ancestry

by Rosemary Levesque

I invite you to set a daily intention for healing. After you offer the intention, journal any new insights, perceptions, or sensations, such as a feeling of lightness or healing.

I ask that I and my ancestors receive only the highest good today. I invite all ancestors, angels and guides of 100% pure love and light to participate in my day through the vibrations of my song and voice. As I prepare to receive these energies, I acknowledge that I am created whole and magnificent. I release all blockages and attachments that give me and my ancestors any illusions away from wholeness and well-being. I intend for complete clearing of old patterns, old beliefs, and the undoing of all that no longer serves me.

___

___

___

___

___

___

___

"Our ancestors and spiritual guides offer a new perspective from their clear point of view." – *The Ancestors Within, Vol 2,* p. 59

"Harmonious sounds create healing, beauty, and grace. Disharmonious sounds create confusion and dis-ease, or patterns away from wholeness and the perfect blueprint of your soul." – *The Ancestors Within, Vol 2,* p. 61

"When you can't get the words out to speak your truth, stand up for who you are and live in health and happiness. It may be time to remember how to sing." – *The Ancestors Within, Vol 2,* p. 62

Thank you for the blessings. I am so happy and grateful to walk my path with you, my ancestors, by my side. Your wisdom, grace, and beauty shine and inspire me to be more fully present, and to manifest higher vibrations of joy in my life. Thank you for your blessings and guidance.

Rosemary Levesque is a licensed spiritual healer trained in vibrational and spiritual energy healing to help you access your innate power to heal – physically, emotionally, and spiritually. She works with detoxification, sound, Reiki, and animals. Rosemary incorporates Shamanic practices in her intuitive classes and healing sessions to heal your spiritual ancestry. Learn more at www.secondnaturehealing.com. Learn how to heal and activate your pineal gland at www.secondnaturehealing.com/pineal-gland-spiritual-enlightenment.

WEEK THIRTY-FOUR

OUR ANCESTORS ARE RELATED

Raising Collective Consciousness

by Leah Skurdal

I invite you to align with God within, a master teacher, or your guardian angel. Then open your heart to a wise, healthy ancestor. Align with the highest good. Ask how you can be of service in healing the family lineage. Ask your wise, healthy ancestor to find a choice point in your family line where your attention could set in motion a higher trajectory and re-calibration for the family line. Listen with your heart wisdom and journal without judgment.

"The father's father's lineage requested release from anger and control issues. This is good for all humanity. We are all related, and the implications reverberate forward in time." – *The Ancestors Within, Vol 2,* p. 68

"Our attention and intention does not necessarily change what really happened, but changes the emotional attachment and the trajectory going forward." – *The Ancestors Within, Vol 2,* p. 69

"As you uplift your own life, you open the doorway for the whole family to be uplifted with you. As you heal your life you create healing for your ancestors and your descendants." – *The Ancestors Within, Vol 2,* p. 70

Thank you, Divine Love expressing through me. I am grateful for this opportunity to serve the highest good. Thank you, Wise Ancestor for guiding me to help my family heal and transform. Thank you for blessing my family with well-being. Blessed Be.

Leah Skurdal is a workshop facilitator, inspirational speaker, and best-selling author. Leah guides people to navigate stress and nurture their bodies by reconnecting to their intuitive inner wisdom. Her transformational workshops and courses awaken the healer within each person to intuit what serves their innate well-being. Learn more at www.leahskurdal.com. Learn the "Healing With Your Ancestors" meditation at www.leahskurdal.com/meditations.

WEEK THIRTY-FIVE

WHEN ANCESTORS ARE SOUL FRIENDS

by Marcia Colver Reichert

Think back through the years. Are there times in your life when your ancestors were definitely there? Do they show their presence in physical ways such as leaving objects, moving things, or playing music for you? Do you hear them speaking in different ways? Do things just pop into your mind, making you wonder where they came from or if it might be an ancestor? Ancestors appear to us because they are our soul friends. Journal about the ways your ancestors reveal themselves to you.

"Ancestors are constantly around me, helping me through whatever happens." – *The Ancestors Within, Vol 2,* p. 75

"The ancestors were nudging me, so I began singing for her, doing my distance healing work, and in my mind, I saw her little spirit sitting alone on a cliff overlooking a beautiful valley in the fairy world, being there."
– *The Ancestors Within, Vol 2,* p. 76

"My grandfather has been feeding me information since he passed, but I didn't recognize it because I refuse to hear voices since his wife and her father, my grandmother and great-grandfather, were institutionalized for that very thing." – *The Ancestors Within, Vol 2,* p. 79

Thank you Spirit for helping me connect with my ancestors, removing anything that stands in the way of my progression in life and for blessing my family in all ways. May I open my ears to hear, open my heart to feel, open my mind to experience all the wonderful gifts my ancestors have to offer me. I am grateful for every experience that comes my way.

Marcia Colver Reichert began life with amazing abilities and perspectives. She travels to spread joy, wonder, and healing to people throughout the world. She is a best-selling author, mentor, shaman, master of healing arts, High Priestess and alchemist. Her goal is to help you "step into your magic." Learn more at www.marciacolver.com. Get access to Marcia's tool from *The Ancestors Within* at www.marciacolver.com/ancestors-within-book.

WEEK THIRTY-SIX

ANGEL MENTORS

Your Connection for Inspiration, Healing, and Love

by Mary Perry

I invite you to begin a meditation practice and to commit to 30 days where you go within to find your wisdom and to allow your angel mentors to lead you to your ancestors. Notice, in the stillness, how you feel. Pay attention to the ideas that present themselves. I invite you to journal about your feelings. Find your "Aha!" moments.

"Is connection to the ancestors something you would love to develop?"
– *The Ancestors Within, Vol 2,* p. 86

"This connection starts you on a journey to go deeper inside to heal past traumas and grow, and to shift energy blocks and move forward in life with ease." – *The Ancestors Within, Vol 2,* p. 86

Offer a blessing. *As I walk this earth today, I bless my ancestors for their strength, courage, faith, and love. Looking in the mirror, my eyes shine the joy and love they send to pave my path. With the deepest gratitude, I send blessings of love and light back to them infused with healing. The cycle is broken as I carry their love in my heart always and leave room in my heart for the angels to dance.*

Rev. Mary Perry is an angel intuitive and healer. She works with her clients in many angelic ways to help them shift limiting beliefs and to help them move forward in their lives. Rev. Mary believes in the magic of love. Learn more at www.wings-unfurled.com. Get access to Mary's tool from *The Ancestors Within* at www.wings-unfurled.com/angel-room.

WEEK THIRTY-SEVEN

A VOICE FROM HOME

Listening to the Call of Your Ancestors

by James Kealiipiilani Kawainui

Take a few minutes to focus on the rhythm of your breath. Let go of the outside world as you turn your attention inwards. Give yourself permission to open the door to your inner home. A short gratitude practice will help you become more in touch with your inner life. Find one or two things you are grateful for in your life. For example, you might say, "I am grateful to be here in this moment, taking time for myself," or "I am grateful to be alive." This moment is about quieting and centering your mind and your energy to hear your inner voice.

Reflect on this "voice from home" experience. What did you hear? What new insights came to you?

____

____

____

____

____

____

"We all have defining moments in our lives when the decision we make alters our course so dramatically that life as we've known it changes forever." – *The Ancestors Within, Vol 2,* p. 91

"I started to hear the voices of the past and felt the presence of my Kūpuna (my ancestors)." – *The Ancestors Within, Vol 2,* p. 93

"Our ancestors are with us all the time. There is never a moment when they are not." – *The Ancestors Within, Vol 2,* p. 94

Thank you, Ancestors, for your presence in my life. I am grateful for your insight, intuition, wisdom, and compassion. Help me to be a better person today than I was yesterday. I am grateful for your strength and guidance. Give me a sign as I move through my day that you are with me. Guide me as I work to overcome the obstacles in my life. Help me live my life with integrity.

James Kawainui is a Native Hawaiian Healer and teacher who is an expert in clearing energetic blockages caused by trauma, injury, and illness. Experience freedom, hope, and clarity in your life. James' passion and commitment is to help people live positive, productive, pain free lives. Learn more at www.jameskawainui.com. Get access to James' tool from *The Ancestors Within* at www.jameskawainui.com/yourancestorwithin.

WEEK THIRTY-EIGHT

FALL EQUINOX

Bonus Chapter
by Ahriana Platten

The Fall Equinox has arrived. It is time to release what no longer serves us and to reflect on what we learned in spring and summer. Now is also the time to honor our ancestors — those upon whose shoulders we stand. Sit with photographs and keepsakes, tell your family stories to younger family members, and fill yourself with gratitude for the gifts of those who dreamed you into being. What ancestors do you honor this year? What have you learned since the year began? What will you release as you move into autumn?

____

____

____

____

____

____

____

____

____

"She looked through my eyes and everything in view seemed to glow."
– *The Ancestors Within,* Vol 1, p. 135

"This was indeed the place of my ancestors. *Why would they leave?* my mother asked out loud. I was wondering the very same thing."
– *The Ancestors Within, Vol 2,* p. 91

"Visiting my ancestral homeland brought me an unexpected gift, a sense that I belong somewhere. – *The Ancestors Within, Vol 1,* p. 138

May the spirit of your ancestors guide you in this season of release. May your choices be wise and healthy, and may you move into the season of reflection with a grateful heart.

Dr. Ahriana Platten is an international speaker, author, and courage builder. She helps people find their purpose and live into it. She's a master ceremonialist and practical mystic, widely appreciated for her authenticity, her professional insights, and her coaching on the process of change. Find more from Ahriana at www.asoulfullworld.com.

WEEK THIRTY-NINE

THE POWER OF YOUR ANCESTORS' PRAYERS

by Frank Byrum

I invite you to connect to the prayers of your ancestors—especially, the prayers said for you. Rely on the knowledge that each prayer is still energetic, still powerful, still alive, still active, and still working. Even if you don't know anything about your origin or feel you cannot claim family prayers, choose a past friend, a past mentor, anyone in your life who has been significant. In your journal, write each name. Then enter into a meditation: relax, breathe deeply, put your hand or hands over your heart. Ask, *What do I need to know right now?* Continue breathing deeply as you listen.

Write about your experience, including your feelings and any messages that came to you.

____

____

____

____

____

____

"Prayer is absolutely generational."
– *The Ancestors Within, Vol 2,* p. 101

"The question remained on my mind and the unknown possibilities swirled. *Why?* is such a hard question." – *The Ancestors Within, Vol 2,* p. 104

"The tool is for you, even if you are adopted or don't know anything about your origin. You can connect to those ancestral prayers and their energy by adding to your daily practice and meditation."
– *The Ancestors Within, Vol 2,* p. 106

After each session, offer a prayer of gratitude and blessings for each ancestor, and remember to pray for those in your life today. Remember that you, too, are a future ancestor of your family, partner, friends, and everyone around you.

Frank has spent the last four decades on a spiritual journey, with a focus on deep self-healing. He earnestly believes everyone can benefit from the foundation of practical daily spiritual practice and that this practice is the best way to "be in the world, but not of the world." Learn more at www.themindfulpathway.com.

WEEK FORTY

CONNECTING THROUGH NATURE'S WISDOM

Bonus Chapter
by Joy Andreasen

Each manifestation of intelligence, whether it is water, air, earth, or fire, has wisdom within. Nature has innate wisdom, and by connecting with aspects of nature we connect with the wisdom of our soul. We are all one, whether we realize it or not. Whatever questions we have about life can be answered through connecting with an aspect of nature.

For the next few days, consciously connect with an aspect of your ancient ancestor, Mother Earth or Father Sky. This may be the sun, the moon, a tree, a bird. Listen for a message. Journal the result.

Sit in silence. Close your eyes. Listen. What do you hear? Try to hear the beating of your heart. Feel the air touching your skin. Listen for nature's wisdom.

"Nature has within it innate wisdom, and by connecting with aspects of nature we connect with the wisdom of our soul."
– *The Ancestors Within, Vol 2,* p. 12

"We are all one, whether we realize it or not. Whatever questions we have about life can be answered through connecting with an aspect of nature."
– *The Ancestors Within, Vol 2,* p. 12

Blessing to our Ancient Ancestors of the Universe: Dear Mother Earth and Father Sky: Thank you for my life. Thank you for allowing me to live and breathe, to laugh and cry. Every blessing I have comes from you. Forgive me for my thoughtless transgressions against you. I will try to live my life realizing the truth of our interconnectedness. Thank you for every moment. Bless you.

Joy Andreasen is an author, psychic, medium, and Shamanic Reiki Energy Healer. With over twenty years' experience delivering messages from the world of Spirit and facilitating healing of the soul, she sees clients and hosts spiritual gatherings via Zoom, phone and face-to-face in her office in Winchester Virginia. Learn more at Joy's website, www.whispersofjoy.net. Find a free ancestral tool at www.whispersofjoy.net/single-post/finding-our-purpose-in-life.

WEEK FORTY-ONE

UNEXPRESSED ANCESTRAL GIFTS

Bonus Chapter
by Marcia Colver Reichert

Wonderful expansion of our creativity and comprehension can occur when we connect with our ancestors on a different level. What unexplored gifts and talents are the ancestors screaming to give to you? Are you seeing the world as they see it now, or are you stuck in a limited understanding of reality? Did tragedy strike one of your ancestors and could you be carrying that wound for them? Were your ancestors condemned for their beliefs and are you carrying a fear of the same? What glorious things could come from releasing those limitations? Are you willing to explore with them?

Consider these questions. Then journal the responses that come to you.

____

____

____

____

____

"Now that I have been embracing and using my psychic gifts rather than chalking them up to my imagination, I liken what I see when I touch someone to an old-time reel-to-reel movie, slowed down so you can see each clip for a split second."
– *The Ancestors Within, Vol 2,* p. 103

"Singing my clients into sacred space and 'snake charming' their energy to help relieve trauma and unlock muscle memory is remarkably effective."
– *The Ancestors Within, Vol 2,* p. 103

"I begin at the ends of the fingers and toes and top of the head and 'gather' the energy in the stomach by continuously moving my hand in a clockwise circle over their stomach, lightly touching so they can feel me 'reeling' the energy in." – *The Ancestors Within, Vol 2,* p. 104

Thank you Spirit for allowing me understanding and connection with my ancestors! I know this will bring many blessings into my life and the world around me. May it also bless the ancestors who were willing to come forward and share their experiences with me. May any discoveries I have made be blessed with healing of wounds and transmutation of energies to love and peace.

Marcia Colver Reichert began life with amazing abilities and perspectives. She travels to spread joy and wonder to the world through her voice. She is a best-selling author, mentor, Shaman, master of healing arts, High Priestess, and channel of song. Her goal is to help you "step into your magic." Learn more at www.marciacolver.com and at www.marciacolver.com/ancestors-within-book

WEEK FORTY-TWO

LETTING GO, EXPANDED

by Arielle

In the very moment you observe, experience, or encounter something that is not desired, the desired is also born into creation and made available to you. The same is true for your understanding of your ancestors, who now seek to co-create with you. As you are journaling here, let go and be open to an uplifted, evolved, fear-free version of your ancestors. Let go and allow a new awareness to reveal itself as the words flow through you onto these pages. Know that your willingness to release your old perspective, something new is created and made available to you.

"For every pattern, for every experience of the undesired, the solution is born into creation at the exact same moment."
– *The Ancestors Within, Vol 2,* p. 133

"You are a creator, and so were your ancestors."
– *The Ancestors Within, Vol 2,* p. 133

"Receive a family bond of the purest of energy, of love, of empowerment; a family bond of freedom." – *The Ancestors Within, Vol 2,* p. 134

Be open to the evolution of your relationships. Be slow to place limits, and quick to allow. Know that if you're perceiving a less than exalted version, there is something better waiting for you. If you're experiencing anything shy of unspeakable joy, there's more awaiting you. Know that you are the ancestor of those to come, and seek only the most exalted version of yourself. Enjoy always!

Arielle of The Collective Consultation is an enthusiastic interpreter of the vibrational communication of the non-physical. As such she hosts interactive consultation sessions for clients with the non-physical aspects of those currently living, those previously physical, as well as the consciousness of infinite intelligence. Learn more at www.thecollectiveconsultation.com.

WEEK FORTY-THREE

WITH EVERY BEAT OF YOUR HEART

by Star Studonivic

I invite you to think about who you are now, in this very moment. Then think of who you were growing up. What shifted in your life circumstances that changed how you are or how you behave in this world? What molded your beliefs? Was there an event or person who changed your way of being? What were the life lessons that changed you? Consider these questions and journal the answers that come to you.

____

____

____

____

____

____

____

____

____

____

____

"Your ancestors are the unseen part of your community, as well as your history." – *The Ancestors Within, Vol 2,* p. 138

"Your connection to Mother Earth is a prelude and introduction to your ancestors who await your visit." – *The Ancestors Within, Vol 2,* p. 138

"So why? Why seek an ancestral connection?"
– *The Ancestors Within, Vol 2,* p. 138

Thank you for allowing me to see who you were. Thank you for wise council, and patience. I honor our connection and hold it sacred. I am grateful for your lineage and life, and I am also grateful to be part of your lineage. Above all, I am grateful for your gentleness and love.

Star Studonivic is a Reiki Master and certified yoga instructor. She is a teacher and conductor of rituals with a lifetime of experience in both leading and tailoring rituals for her clients. She is also a writer and calligrapher. Find Star and learn more at www.studonivic.com.

WEEK FORTY-FOUR

EMBRACING ANCESTRAL CHAOS

by Adriana Smith

Understand that I am a woman with autism, and I am learning as I write! You have a voice to help reach others, so I ask you to use your voice to help me share my message.

We are connected with our ancestors. The ancestors that are around us and within us are calling us for assistance. They are affected by energies that shouldn't be. They are stuck within this universe and within this earth, and they don't have a way out except through us.

I counsel these ancestors, and I encourage you to support your ancestors, too. Try to understand their problems and bring insight to them so they can understand more and find healing that will free them.

Which of your ancestors comes to mind as you read these ideas? What are the struggles, issues, or patterns that keep that ancestor stuck? Ask them questions, and journal your answers. How can you help them heal and move on?

Do not judge the ideas that come to you as you write; just let them flow. Then bring your own insight and perspective to your ancestors' struggles by including your perspective. See your own light shining into their darkness to increase movement, energy, and healing.

"All you need to do is be nice and have patience for yourself and others. Your energy is not just your energy; it is shared energy that thrives from moving forward. If you can move it, do it."
– *The Ancestors Within, Vol 2,* p. 149

Please really feel the power of kindness and practice kindness always. Just love to smile and receive smiles. People, OMG, this is communication at its finest.

Adriana loves to help others. She works behind the scenes, using energy to shift reality into new possibilities, and she is a camera-friendly visual for other non-speakers. Find Adriana and learn more at www.sharonsweb.com.

WEEK FORTY-FIVE

EMPATHS AND ANCESTORS

Cultivating Empathic Skills to Connect and Work with Your Ascendants

by Elizabeth R. Kipp

As humans, we are all empaths. Some of us can discern empathy more profoundly and on a more subtle level than others. Some of us are highly sensitive empaths. It is possible for empaths to develop skills that allow us to experience others neutrally, so we do not take their energy onto ourselves. When working with ancestral energies, it is helpful to cultivate empathic skills and allow yourself to feel, but not become attached to, these vibrations.

Ask yourself when your empathic nature has left you too open to the energy of others. Develop a visualization that will support your ability to feel with others but not become attached to their vibrations. Journal about an experience of taking on too much of another's feelings. Then journal about the visualization that will help you prevent this in the future.

____

____

____

____

"In developing a relationship with and connecting to your ancestors, holding space allows you to open yourself to experience whatever is revealed to you in the moment and be present without any expectation of what you might discover." – *The Ancestors Within, Vol 2,* p. 155

"By remaining in a neutral position physically, mentally, and intuitively and by staying in the present moment without any expectation of an outcome, you allow yourself to open and receive any transmissions your ancestors wish to share with you." – *The Ancestors Within, Vol 2,* p. 156

"As we do the work to clear burdens, unresolved issues carried to us by our ancestors, the Ancestral Clearing® process is alchemizing because we are transmuting one experience, one burden, into another – liberation from that burden." – *The Ancestors Within, Vol 2,* p. 158

Once you have mastered grounding, holding space, and deep listening—and once you understand the concept of taking on the energy of others—you can begin to communicate with your ancestors. The form of communication can be any that makes sense to you. My favorite way to commune with my ancestors is through the process of Ancestral Clearing®, a method of connecting with the ancestors and releasing any unresolved burden remaining in the lineage.

Elizabeth Kipp is a chronic pain specialist, yoga-informed addiction recovery coach, Ancestral Clearing® Practitioner, yoga and meditation teacher, and international best-selling author of *The Way Through Chronic Pain: Tools to Reclaim Your Healing Power*. She focuses on helping people realize the power of their inherent healing at www.elizabeth-kipp.com.

WEEK FORTY-SIX

WHAT'S POSSIBLE

Purifying Ancestral Energies

by Rev. Devi Grace

Find a secret nature spot where you feel you have space for the magic of life to reveal itself. Bring with you a candle, fire bowl, cedar or incense, a pen and paper, your favorite family prayers, a glass of water, and a willing heart.

Ask and imagine that the fire element represents your dynamic masculine qualities of truth and that the water element represents your intuitive feminine side. This creates a paired alchemy for transmutation. Ponder your own self-healing ability as you request that this meditative space be cleansed. Write a letter thanking your ancestors for the purification of energies that no longer serve you so that you can discover what's possible.

____

____

____

____

____

"With El (sacred male) and Asherah (divine female) - close your eyes and welcome these two masculine and feminine principles to over-light your entire body, every cell, atom, molecule, and particle of your being."
– *The Ancestors Within, Vol 2,* p. 165

"The Father (Alpha) and his holy mirror the Mother (Omega) are secret passwords for your direct access or pin codes into this eternal first creation pathway of divine regeneration." – *The Ancestors Within, Vol 2,* p. 166

"Please take yourself into the simple textures of all this wisdom, and come back to how you can comfortably nestle down into the trunk of this Ancestral Tree of Life that specifically has your name on it, carved for you by the one that created your eternal soul."
– *The Ancestors Within, Vol 2,* p. 166

Silently acknowledge the water as the womb space of your Supernal Mother and recognize the lit candle as the spark of life from your Supernal Father. Give thanks to them for washing the family line inside of you, and light your paper message with an offering from the earth (such as sage.) See the ashes of your knowing rise to release the old pressures of your past conformity or hidden unhealthy loyalties, and welcome the rebirth of your sovereign being. Line up the flickering flame with the liquid water in your field of view and ask them (Holy Mom and Dad) to reconcile the main male/female issues in your body with gratitude.

As a seasoned multiple near-death experience facilitator and embodied leadership trainer for over 15 years, Reverend Devi Grace specializes in supporting awakened luminaries to integrate the synthesis of all of their lifetimes. She initiates global messengers in the ancient art and science of masculine/feminine alchemy for the cultural transformation of divine human consciousness. Find her and her work at:
www.spreaker.com/show/divine-union-transmissions
www.speakingtreeoflife.com
www.divineunionacademy.com
www.divineunionfoundation.org.

WEEK FORTY-SEVEN

DIVINE HEALING THROUGH THE TENTH CHAKRA

Accessing the Gifts of Our Ancestors

by Jill Sonnek

An ancestral pathway I refer to is often called the "Tenth Chakra" or "Earth Star." It is located around 18 inches below the feet. This ancestral gateway is one of the keys to healing the dis-ease and traumas carried in epigenetics. *Epigenetics*, literally meaning "above the genetics," are the ancestral memories carried in our DNA. Each of us can tap into the lessons of our ancestors from the Tenth Chakra. Through this pathway, we can re-wire our DNA, turning on and off our genes.

Three fantastic resources exist here. When working at its peak, the Tenth Charka pulls three energy sources from below: the gifts of our ancestors, the earth's help, and our Divine heritage. It draws from both the male and female ancestors. It also can pull every element found on Earth. Most importantly, we can tap into Divine energy.

Open yourself to the energy of the tenth chakra and the wisdom it offers. Journal about the insights you receive.

____

____

____

____

"The goal of energy healing is to create clear energetic pathways bringing in the best energy for your highest good."
– *The Ancestors Within, Vol 2,* p. 173

"We can rewrite our legacy through the Tenth Chakra by transforming those [painful ancestral] lessons from fear into lessons learned in love."
– *The Ancestors Within, Vol 2,* p. 175

"If you acknowledge the shadow or negative quality,
you can find and turn on the gift." – *The Ancestors Within, Vol 2,* p. 175

Focus on what you have written. Write down the new words, one below the other. Visualize them as two parts of a whole. Focus on balancing the two together like yin and yang. Draw an arrow from one to the other. Thank your ancestors for these gifts. Ask for their assistance in rebalancing. You may find my audio meditation, listed in the link below, to be helpful.

Jill Sonnek is an Energy Medicine Practitioner who lives with her family in Minneapolis, Minnesota. Jill believes that all healing comes from accepting Divine Love. She has a unique ability to connect her clients to that Divine energy. Learn more at www.streamsofgrace.net/ancestors-within-meditation http://www.streamsofgrace.net.

WEEK FORTY-EIGHT

YOU ARE THE ANTIDOTE

The Power of Speaking Blessings into Your Lineage

by Darlene de la Plata

Reflection is a powerful catalyst for change. Taking a few minutes every day to reflect on three simple areas can help you begin to craft a legacy that puts a smile on your face every night when you go to sleep.

First, know that your choices affect the distant future; make decisions with the end in mind. Do your actions carry the frequency of success? Second, visualize the future. Imagine a conversation with your great-grandchildren where they are enjoying a legacy where you laid the groundwork. Feel the love and gratitude. And third, apply this creative power to improve the quality of your daily life. Live with intention, use life-giving words, and pay it forward. Sleep. Wake. Repeat. You are the antidote.

Write about your experiences living with the future of your family in mind, becoming the antidote.

____

____

____

____

____

"Every choice you make today will impact your family for multiple generations." – *The Ancestors Within, Vol 2,* p. 208

"When your focus is helping future generations, the universe will conspire to have your back." – *The Ancestors Within, Vol 2,* p. 208

"We have everything we need inside of us to create the version of ourselves we dream of being." – *The Ancestors Within, Vol 2,* p. 209

Prayer to Honor the Ancestors: *Life is a more beautiful and abundant experience because you sowed seeds of blessings into my future. I am forever grateful for the prayers you imparted to me before I was born. I pray our future generations will continue to be blessed with long life, health, prosperity, children, safety, and true joy, and may they always use God's creative power of intentional words to bless the generations to come. Amen.*

Darlene, "The Herbmom," de la Plata is an ordained minister, fierce health warrior, visionary coach, best-selling author, amazon explorer, wealth strategist, and professional muse. She is always in the right place at the right time with all the right people and helps clients find their joy and live their dreams. Learn more at www.theherbmom.com.

WEEK FORTY-NINE

LOVE MAKES YOU A HERO

Opening the Gateways for All to Heal

by Melissa Jolly Graves

Thank you for being here and present at this moment. Your ancestors have long awaited the time when you could communicate with them. This is not just any journal, for the words you write in this book will become a gateway to consciousness. Be raw, be real, face the truth, write letters to ghosts, really let go of any outside thoughts and just write what comes to you. Your ancestors need journaling, too. Take this opportunity to get to know yourself, because you are the most precious thing that you and your ancestors have at this exact moment. Ask your ancestors how you can best use this gateway to consciousness. Your love makes you their hero.

"You are the present moment and the star that keeps hope in your DNA."
– *The Ancestors Within, Vol 2,* p. 195

"Being a hero doesn't mean you have to fix the outside world."
– *The Ancestors Within, Vol 2,* p. 192

"We are not individuals; we are quantum particles of this entire universe."
– *The Ancestors Within, Vol 2,* p. 194

It is time to end this chapter in your life and embark on a new adventure through your heart. Before you turn the page, take time to reflect your most honorable traits. Allow the memories of love, laughter, passion, happiness, and comfort to hold a space in your heart. Invite your ancestors into that space and surrender to the healing and love surrounding you.

Melissa is an exceptional seer, who strives to offer people a new perspective on life. Her accomplishments include being a successful wife, mother, and business owner of Euphoric Source. As a teacher, counselor, minister, author, public speaker, and documentarian Melissa opens the hearts and minds of many. Learn more at www.euphoricsource.com.

WEEK FIFTY

HEAL YOURSELF AND YOUR FAMILY FROM INHERENT GENERATIONAL TRAUMA

The Truth Will Set You Free

by Crystal Rasmussen

Inherent family trauma will keep you struggling with some of the same issues over and over again. It will affect the choices you make, your thoughts, your emotions, your health, your daily experiences, and how you perceive the world. I invite you to pause and observe your own family. What beliefs, emotions, limitations, thoughts, behaviors, characteristics and physical ailments do you recognize? Write them down. Where do you feel they originated? What if you knew these might be unhealed traumas passed down from generation to generation as an energetic code within your family lineage and that these can be healed? What would change for you?

____

____

____

____

____

____

"Inherent family trauma will keep you struggling with some of the same issues over and over again." – *The Ancestors Within, Vol 2,* p. 201

"Imagine the ripple effect of healing that can take place for you, your own family, across the planet, and all of humanity by releasing and healing the pain and suffering that has been passed down from generations."
– *The Ancestors Within, Vol 2,* p. 202

"You are a culmination of all your ancestors that have walked before you, both the pain and the gifts." – *The Ancestors Within, Vol 2,* p. 203

As you recognize the patterns that continue to get passed down from one generation to the next, you begin to realize that there is nothing wrong with you. You recognize there is unhealed trauma within your ancient bloodline. The most beautiful part is that the ancestors are ready, willing, and available to support you and your family in healing.

Crystal Rasmussen is a Generational Healing® Teacher and Spiritual Guide. Her goal is to support you in releasing pain and suffering from your ancient bloodline that is stored within your genetic lineage and to heal you. As a Generational Healer®, she teaches women to communicate with their ancestors, awaken their spiritual gifts, and heal inherent family trauma. Learn more at her website, www.crystalrasmussen.com.

WEEK FIFTY-ONE

THE SONG OF THE SPIRITS

by Jesse Barrientez

I invite you to expand your horizons and open your mind to a Native American perspective that was almost exterminated. Most people think the chiefs were the leaders. People thought that because men were always in front, they were the apparent leaders. The reality is women are the portal between worlds. Women made a lot of our decisions and, more importantly, they made us. We were disposable—the reason we stood in front of our women. Women have the ability to bring us back with their gift of giving life. As men, we don't have that ability.

Take time to meditate about the gifts of women and men. How are we different? How are we the same? Consider your own balance between masculine and feminine energy? How do these energies manifest in your life?

"A lot of People say they can't choose where they come from, but the reality is that we choose our destination from the start."
– *The Ancestors Within, Vol 2,* p. 207

"I learned about our dreams and how the ancestors talk to us through them." – *The Ancestors Within, Vol 2,* p. 208

"There is no heaven (happy hunting grounds, Nirvana, Shambhala) if there is no earth, and vice versa." – *The Ancestors Within, Vol 2,* p. 209

I am blessed to learn these teachings from my ancestors. I am humbled to share them with you, and I am grateful to share them with future generations. These teachings would be lost if they were not shared and passed on, as I am sharing them and passing them on to you. They say, "ignorance is bliss." I say now that you know, what are you going to do with your knowledge?

Jesse Barrientez is a singer-songwriter, poet, author, and Anishinaabe man. He is the CEO of Everything Art, where he teaches people the beauty of life through artistic expression. He is a co-founder of The 7th Generation Group, where indigenous youth are brought together with the offering of insight and the expression of the love we have when we are together as one. Please view the YouTube video titled "Put Your Asehmaa Out" and find Jesse on Facebook at "MoneyDoo."

WEEK FIFTY-TWO

CHANNELING THE ANCESTORS

Breath – Voice -- Truth

by Lore Ross

This week I invite you on a journey of Breath - Voice - Truth. Each breath brings connection — connection to body, self, and your ancestral lineage. Each breath awakens your connection with your Ancestors. It takes courage to step into alignment and balance. It takes bravery to feel your breath and to trust your body. It takes strength to believe in the language of your own Voice. It takes power to let that Truth speak through you.

Follow these steps, slowly and with care. Then journal your experiences:

1. Sit, stand, or lie down.
2. Turn on the alarm or timer for 30 seconds to 5 minutes.
3. Place one hand on your heart.
4. Place the other hand on your belly.
5. Close your eyes.
6. Inhale.
7. Exhale.
8. Feel your body as it breathes.

Journal your results. How did you feel during this exercise? Remember, being present in the presence is simply one breath at a time.

____

____

"All we truly need is—quite literally and theoretically—to take one breath at a time." – *The Ancestors Within, Vol 2,* p. 217

"Voice is action. It is an alignment and way of being in the world."
– *The Ancestors Within, Vol 2,* p. 218

"Your truth. It is the language born in, and of, your heart."
– *The Ancestors Within, Vol 2,* p. 219

Thank you for joining me on this journey. May you feel each breath as it passes through you. May you allow the wisdom of your own voice to be spoken and heard. May you always walk with the knowledge of your truth. Wishing you beautiful moments of connection and presence in your own body as you step into the world.

Lore Ross is an expert ancestral channel and intuitive. Healing through language and sound, she serves the global population to create transformation and awareness. Her work centers on how to rewrite the body™ and heal stories of personal, ancestral, and global trauma and grief, creating movement forward and transformative lightness through ancient dialects, sound, and song. Aligned with Source, she offers a gentle, non-directed approach to healing and transformation for trauma, grief, illness, and injury, as well as offering insight and guidance. Learn more at www.rewritetheobdy.org.

A LETTER TO OUR READERS

Thank you for your willingness to discover, engage, and embrace your ancestors by using this journal. Whether this was your first time journaling, or whether you experimented with a new method, we hope that you have opened pathways to the ancestors who came before you and who live on within you.

What brought you to this journal? Perhaps you felt cut off from your ancestors, due to a lack of documents, because you were adopted, or even because one of your ancestors was a foundling. You may have had no connections with or knowledge of your ancestors, only your own experiences, talents, and interests, along with your face looking back from the mirror.

Maybe you had genealogy records going back hundreds of years or had DNA results telling you where your ancestors had lived during a certain time…but you were stuck in your ancestral research. One thing is for sure, you had the desire to know more about your ancestors—who they were, where they lived, what they were about, and how they show up in your life. No matter how little or how much information you had when you started this book, you have more now: techniques, clues, perceptions, even answers or pathways to uncover them.

Our authors dug deep within themselves to find prompts that would help you ignite new relationships or establish a deeper connection with your ancestors and a deeper understanding of your life. Each author had a sincere desire that readers would experience an "Aha!" moment or a monumental shift in awareness, along with a new sensitivity and a greater understanding of the many ways you can discover and connect with your ancestors. Each of us tried to help you discover insight and experiences that you can't wait to share with present and future generations of your family.

We'd love to hear your feedback and experience with the tools and prompts. Please share your reviews on Amazon, and on "The Ancestors Within" Facebook Group.

Your ancestors call you to your best life, your best experiences, and your best connection to them. Most of all, they're calling you to the person you were born to become. Your story is an ever changing novel of you!

Your ancestors have waited your whole life for this moment…*and your next!*

Love,

The Authors

ACKNOWLEDGMENTS

AN OVERFLOW OF GRATITUDE

Your ancestors have waited your whole life for this moment… for you to reach out to them, for you to seek them from inside yourself and the experiences of your life. You have fulfilled their dream with your engagement with this journal, recording your interactions with them and lovingly scribing your greatest experiences in this book, for those who come after you.

When I drew my heart-map on January 6, 2021, I had no vision of the books, the magazine articles, the podcasts, and the interviews that would happen in the ensuing ten months of 2021. I was simply taking dictation – taking the heartfelt messages of my ancestors and a Divine web of international need for each of us to reach for our ancestral connection.

When I'm doing ancestral eye readings it is often brought to me that the person I'm reading would not live the way they do if they knew who their ancestors were – kings, heroes, gurus, masters, artisans – if they knew all the details of who they have been, if they knew the details they carry within.

Thank you. Thank you for being willing to try some new methods of opening your own doors of discovery. Just as in the 2000's we are finding forgotten artifacts beneath our oceans, deserts, and even in our jungles, you have begun to find forgotten gifts and memories, stored within you.

Huge thank you to our amazing authors who went back into their chapters of *The Ancestors Within* to choose the best of their quotes and prompts for you to use as you seek your ancestors. Their chapters, tools, and online resources are an amazing gift to our world, for you to use and experience.

Thank you to my amazing editor, Cheri Colburn, for every adjustment and correction—and for helping us share message and serve our readers.

This journal wouldn't be here if not for the love and support of my wonderful husband, Daniel, who listens to my ideas, supports me in late nights of working, and understands the shifts in my work that are Divinely guided.

Tremendous thanks to my adopted family, for teaching me to respect and seek my elders, to love my grandparents, for their support of my creative gifts in writing, and music, and for tolerating so many of my musings, which must have seemed so foreign to them.

Huge thanks to my biological family for allowing me back into your lives, and tolerating my many questions about my ancestry and linking of clues and synchronicities and connections.

Thank you to my ancestors. I've waited my whole life for THIS moment

ABOUT THE AUTHOR

Amy Gillespie Dougherty

Founder of *Irigenics*® Ancestral Eye Reading and CLARA (Children's Lives Are the Responsibility of All)

Amy is a results-driven innovator, speaker, and bestselling author with more than twenty years' experience creating impactful self-discovery, awareness, and life-coaching programs.

Amy's corporate experience in systems performance and disaster relief proved invaluable in her work to create survival skills programs for children and disadvantaged families in third-world countries. She received accolades from USAID and the US Embassy for training programs she created in Mozambique, through her nonprofit TIOS (Treinemento Internacional para os Orfáos e sua Sobrevivéncia; International Training for Orphans and Their Survival), which is now known as CLARA: Children's Lives Are the Responsibility of All.

Thriving as a trailblazer, Amy returned to the U.S. to create *Irigenics*® Ancestral Eye Reading. The organization was originally developed as a survival skills program because the technique helps to reduce self-destructive behaviors, including suicide patterns, in teens and young adults.

Amy believes in the power of the ancestral pulse within each of us, and she believes in our ability to reach the best of our best. She has directly helped thousands of people understand *the rest of their story* by interpreting their ancestral and epigenetic patterns. She's given motivational speeches and interactive self-discovery workshops at Boys and Girls Club and the Department of Corrections. Amy does all of this with one goal in mind: To create new programs and systems that guide young adults to an earlier sense of life purpose, along with the ability to become the person they were born to become.

Amy now teaches Irigenics Ancestral Eye Reading, an innovative self-discovery approach, to holistic practitioners to help them uncover their clients' true gifts and talents. She's inspired to continue teaching practitioners to recognize and assess ancestral information to support their clients in their efforts to reach their full potential for healing and thriving. She helps practitioners move from being *one of the many*—offering traditional self-discovery and self-healing techniques—to being *the one* who uses this dynamic method to interpret clients' ancestral patterns.

If you want to become *THE ONE* to take your clients to the next level with *Irigenics*® Ancestral Eye Reading, visit the website: www.irigenics.com/application-to-train-in-ancestral-eye-reading.

OTHER BOOKS BY THE AUTHOR AMY GILLESPIE DOUGHERTY

The Ancestors Within Volumes 1 and 2

The Ancestors Within series was founded with the mission to help readers understand that a direct relationship with their ancestors is not just possible: it already resists. All of us are born with a certain number of unresolved traumas we can heal, along with a certain number of gifts we can express, create from, and share with the world. This is true even if we are adopted and have no idea who are ancestors are. In fact, this may even be more true when we have no idea who are ancestors are. Learn why your ancestors have waited your whole life for THIS moment…

Volume 1—The Ancestors Within: Reveal & Heal The Ancient Memories You Carry

Amy brings together 25 author-experts in the area of repeat ancestral patterns. From planting a family tree to writing your own family decree, from autism to adoption, this book gives you an amazing array of new tools and perspectives for recognizing and understanding how repeat familial patterns may be showing up in your life. Each of the authors offers online interactive tools for you to recognize your ancestral repeat patterns.

In Amy's chapter, "Chapter 1: The Adoptees Dream: Recognizing Your Ancestors in a *Whole* New Way," she introduces you to a number of tools you can use to recognize your ancestors within, especially if you don't know who your ancestors are (due to your own adoption or due to an ancestor's adoption, re-homing or another kind of displacement from their original family and identity). You will leave this chapter with a newfound respect for your genetic family and, for whom it is relevant, your adopted family, recognizing that they have played a key role in providing you with tne experiences and healing tools beyond what your ancestors had.

Volume 2—The Ancestors Within: Reveal & Connect With Your Ancient Origins

Amy brings forth the work of 25 author-experts, compiling methods developed over the course of more than 250 years for discovering and connecting with your ancestors. Special emphasis is placed on readers who either don't know their ancestors or who know enough to wish they weren't related. The book provides tools and techniques for helping readers resolve problematic patterns.

In Amy's chapter, "Chapter 1: The Ancestral Key: Unlocking the DVD of Your Ancestors," she introduces you to the amazing DVD you already have in the irises of your eyes, and she helps you to begin decoding this information. You can't play a cassette in an 8-track tape deck, and you can't decode the information revealed in the DVD of your eyes (including images of your ancestors) without the right decoder. Amy's online ancestral tools include information that will help you take your own eye photos, and her chapter provides information to help you interpret the images, helping you begin the journey of discovering your ancestors within.

The Ultimate Guide To Self-Healing, Volume 4

Amy is the author of Chapter 6 in this book, "Resolving Cellular Memory: Your Ancestors Have Waited Your Whole Life for THIS Moment." She takes you on a journey into the deepest cellular memories of your life… your in-utero experiences, by having you meet your birthparents before you were conceived. Her audio tool will guide you through this walking visualization exercise to reset your internal dialogue by establishing a compassionate understanding of the first moments of the creation of you.

The Lost Scribe: Forgotten Channel Of The Ancients

The Lost Scribe is the first fiction book in the Maddie Clare Owens (MCO) series, a collection of novels Amy is co-writing with her husband Daniel Dougherty. This book embraces Amy's experiences working in Guatemala as part of her survival skills training programs, including a deeply channeled message from Melchiezedek about the workings of the Universe. *The Lost Scribe* seamlessly weaves together fiction and nonfiction, as Maddie Clare Owens finds herself thrown into a world of mysticism, corruption, and danger, not knowing whom to trust. Amy and Daniel look forward to publishing the next MCO Book, which embraces the world of intricate ancestral synchronicities in our current lives.

Six Years In Mozambique: Things I Haven't Told Mom

Six Years in Mozambique is the autobiographical account of Amy's six years creating survival skills training programs in Sub-Saharan Africa. As a 39-year-old woman with no experience in aid work, HIV prevention, or even foreign languages, Amy forged forward to create life-saving skills programs in six orphan projects and schools in Mozambique. *Six Years* takes you on a breathless ride through the realities and grit of aid work in Africa, where using your common sense can effect huge changes in the lives of children.

To learn more about Amy's books, visit her website: www.amygillespie.com.

Made in the USA
Monee, IL
23 November 2021